the Weekend Crafter®

Woodcarving

the
Weekend
Crafter®

Woodcarving

20 Great Projects for Beginners & Weekend Carvers

JOHN HILLYER

LARK BOOKS

A Division of Sterling Publishing Co., Inc.
New York

Editor: Joe Rhatigan

Art Director: Dana Irwin

Cover Design: Barbara Zaretsky

Photography: Sandra Stambaugh

Illustrations: Orrin Lundren

Assistant Art Director: Hannes Charen

Editorial Assistance: Heather Smith, Nathalie Mornu

Production Assistance: Shannon Yokeley

10 9 8 7 6 5 4

Published by Lark Books, A Division of
Sterling Publishing Co., Inc.
387 Park Avenue South, New York, N.Y. 10016

© 2002, John Hillyer

Distributed in Canada by Sterling Publishing,
c/o Canadian Manda Group, 165 Dufferin Street
Toronto, Ontario, Canada M6K 3H6

Distributed in the U.K. by
Guild of Master Craftsman Publications Ltd.,
Castle Place, 166 High Street, Lewes, East Sussex, England BN7 1XU
Tel: (+ 44) 1273 477374, Fax: (+ 44) 1273 478606,
e-mail: pubs@thegmcgroup.com, Web: www.gmcpublications.com

Distributed in Australia by Capricorn Link (Australia) Pty Ltd.,
P.O. Box 704, Windsor, NSW 2756 Australia

If you have questions or comments about this book, please contact:
Lark Books
67 Broadway
Asheville, NC 28801
(828) 253-0467

Manufactured in China

ISBN: 1-57990-248-0

For information about custom editions, special sales, premium
and corporate purchases, please contact Sterling Special Sales
Department at 800-805-5489 or specialsales@sterlingpub.com.

Acknowledgments

There is neither enough time nor pages in this book to thank the many
carvers, friends, and students who gave me encouragement and influenced
my woodcarving experience, but I would like to acknowledge the following:

■ My grandfather, Irving Finch, who encouraged me in my earliest
woodcarving endeavors
■ My scoutmaster, Warren de Brown, who signed my woodcarving merit
badge in 1938
■ The many carvers and students who shared their time and talents and
knowledge so generously
■ Chip Chats Magazine, which has provided inspiration, information, and
knowledge over the years
■ Woodcarver Rick Butz, who turned on my creative juices during a
weekend
workshop and motivated the launching of my professional carving career
■ G. B. Chiltoskey and his wife Mary, who inspired me to submit my
carvings for jurying into the Southern Highland Craft Guild
■ Woodcarver Helen Gibson, who made it possible to be part of the John C.
Campbell Folk School experience
■ Woodcarver Harold Enlow, who introduced me to caricature carving in a
workshop at the Vesterheim Norwegian-American Museum in Decorah,
Iowa
■ The Western North Carolina Woodcarving Club members who exhibited
support and encouragement for this venture
■ My editor, Joe Rhatigan, who guided my efforts in the literary world, and
Dana Irwin, who put together a fabulous book
■ Sandra Stambaugh, who did a terrific job of photography for the book
■ And my wife June for her enthusiastic support and patient understanding
during this writing experience, for putting up with the wood chips tracked
into the house, and for her valued critique of my carving efforts

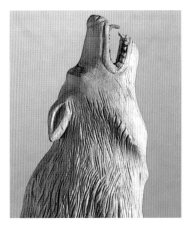

CONTENTS

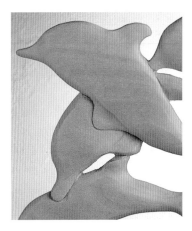

INTRODUCTION

At the age of 13, I received my Boy Scout merit badge in woodcarving, and I've been hooked ever since. In fact, I can barely remember a time when I haven't been carving. I have also taught woodcarving to folks from all walks of life, and it's always a joy to watch others create carvings they thought were beyond them.

Woodcarving is an ancient art found in every corner of the world in every culture. Examples of the many styles of carving include whittling, incised carving, chip carving, pierced carving, relief carving, in-the-round carving (sculpture), and architectural carving. You'll find examples of these in this book. Each project is designed to aid you in learning the basic techniques and in working toward becoming a good woodcarver, while building self-confidence and satisfaction with your progress and your work.

The basics section reviews the skills and techniques of woodcarving and includes a simple project to introduce you to the four phases involved in carving. Use this section as a guide and/or reference as you work on the projects. Feel free to experiment and make changes to the design patterns, or create your own.

Woodcarving is a creative activity in which you can develop your own design while having a lot of fun. Like other hobbies, you'll find that woodcarving can become addictive, consuming hours of your time, while increasing your joy of living. Some of these projects may require more than a weekend at first; but as you gain knowledge and experience using your tools, the execution and quality of your work will improve. Most of all, you'll have fun. So relax and enjoy the wood-carving experiences in this book.

Woodcarving is fun, anyway you cut it.

John Hillyer

TOOLS

The first question most beginning carvers ask is, "What tools do I need to get started?" You really only need a few tools when you start carving, and instead of buying a complete carving set, purchase tools as you need them. Usually, when you buy a set you don't save any money, plus, you end up with some tools you rarely use. Buy the best quality you can afford; good, pre-sharpened, high-carbon steel tools will save you money in the long run.

Purchasing tools by catalog or over the Internet can be difficult since you can't feel the tool to see if it's a good fit for you and your project. There are woodcarving stores that provide tools, books, blanks, and other carving supplies. See page 80 for more information on suppliers.

Knives

You'll need a good knife—one that feels good in your hand. There are three types to choose from: a folding blade (pocket knife), a fixed-blade (bench knife), or an interchangeable blade knife. I prefer a fixed-blade knife primarily because it's safer. There are also many blade shapes and styles in a variety of steels. Select a high-carbon steel blade with a hardness of RC 55 to 60. It will hold its edge longer than a stainless steel blade or low-carbon steel blade. For general carving, roughing out, and shaping I prefer a blade about 5/32 inch (4 mm) thick and 1½ to 2 inches (3.8 to 5.1 cm) long. A smaller narrower blade is better for detail work. A Kolrosing knife has a small blade and is used to incise.

Some carvers prefer the interchangeable blade knife because it uses disposable blades, eliminating the need to resharpen the blade when it loses its edge. Another good feature is that this knife handle can be used with some small gouges as well.

Gouges

Gouges come in a variety of widths and sweeps (curvatures). The sweep is denoted by a number. The flatter the curvature, the lower the number. Thus a #3 gouge is almost flat compared to a #11 U-shaped veiner. Obviously, a #10 or #11 gouge will make a deeper cut and remove more wood than a #3 gouge. On the other hand, the #3

gouge will give you a smoother finishing cut. The V-tool, or #12 gouge, is available in a number of different angles, from 24° to 90°. The most common angles are 60° to 70°.

CLOCKWISE FROM THE TOP: an interchangeable knife, a curved knife, two fixed-blade knives, and disposable blades and gouges for the interchangeable knife

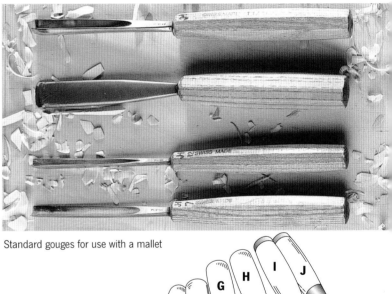

Standard gouges for use with a mallet

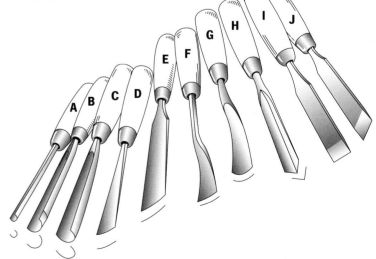

FIGURE 1: Gouges and Their Cutting Lines: A & B. Veiners; C. Deep Sweep; D. Fishtail; E. Straight; F. Spoon; G. Long Bend; H. V-tool; I. Firmer; J. Skew

Choose gouges with handles that don't easily roll when laid on your work surface. (You'll spend less time repairing damaged cutting edges due to the tools rolling off the table.)

Keep in mind the size and type of carving you want to do when selecting your gouges. For handheld work, palm gouges are more convenient than standard gouges. Micro-gouges are needed for miniature work. Sculptures and large carvings, as well as relief carvings, require standard gouges with heavier handles to withstand pounding with a mallet.

Saws

Woodcarvers use a number of saws depending on the task, though a coping saw is probably the most common one used. It uses replaceable high-carbon steel blades, fitted in a steel frame with a handle. It can be used to cut narrow curves, though it requires a degree of patience to keep

TOP: drawknife; **BOTTOM:** scorp

the blade from breaking or bending. You can also use it with a fret board to cut out your designs (see page 10). Another useful saw is the backsaw, which can be used to help cut out waste wood.

Specialty Cutting Tools

These tools are not necessary for the projects in this book, but they may come in handy for some specific tasks.

A draw knife is used to remove bark or for fast rough removal of wood, as in shaping long pieces for furniture. A scorp is a type of knife with a curved, circular blade that's ideal for scooping out bowls, spoons, or masks.

Abrasive Tools

Files and rasps remove waste wood quickly and smoothly. They come in coarse, medium, and fine filing cuts. Flat, half round, and round shapes are available—always use them with handles. Rifflers are double-ended files or rasps that come in a wide variety of shapes. Use them for getting into tight corners and hard-to-reach places to remove small slivers of wood. Sanding sticks that use

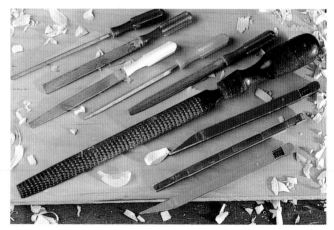

A variety of files

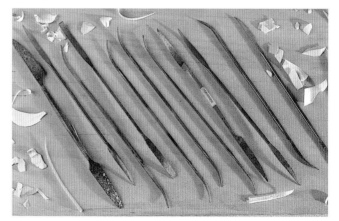

Assorted rifflers

Sanding tools

small sanding belts also help get into the tight spots to smooth out small, rough areas. A flexible sander is excellent for curved surfaces. Drum sanders for use in drill presses and hand drills, as well as sanding stars and flapper sanders, are a big help in finish sanding. Sanding mediums come in a wide variety of grits and materials to meet any need. I prefer cloth-backed abrasives or open abrasives. I also use flexible plastic pads for final smoothing. Use sandpaper only after you've finished carving—the loosened particles of abrasive become lodged in the wood and will quickly dull your tools.

Power Tools

If and when you begin to make your own blanks (the roughed out design) in quantities, a bandsaw is indispensable. The large selection of blades allows you to make difficult cuts with ease, far surpassing anything you can do with a coping saw and a fret board. A jigsaw can do inside cuts, but is limited in the thickness of stock it can handle. Belt, disc, and flapper sanders are helpful in the finishing operations as well as for removing bark. Many carvers use rotary tools with a wide variety of bits to carve details, such as feathers. There are handheld grinders, flexible shaft units, and small high-speed (35,000 rpm) micro-motor carvers. There are also at least four reciprocating power gouge carvers available today that make it possible for carvers with arthritic hands and "tennis elbows" to continue to carve.

Drum sanders and diamond bits

Clockwise from top: spring clamp, carver's screw, vise, quick clamp, and carver's glove

Holding Devices

If you use a vise to clamp your carving, use one that has jaws that won't mark your carving (or fasten a waste block to your work before putting it in the vise). I have often used a ¼-inch (6 mm) lag screw with a washer and a wing nut to fasten my carving to the bench. You may want to use a carver's glove of coated steel wire to protect your non-carving hand while holding your piece. I have a longtime carving friend who wears a heavy leather apron to protect himself when he carves against his chest. When finishing or painting your pieces you may want to use an awl or painting stick screwed into the bottom of your project.

FRET BOARD

To help support your wood as you cut out your blank with a coping saw, I suggest you make a fret board, which is a simple board that supports the wood while you saw it. Simply clamp it to your bench or table, and hold your cop-

A fret board on top of a bench hook

ing saw vertically in the "V" as you cut out your blank. See figure 2 for the fret board dimensions.

BENCH HOOK

If you plan on doing any relief or in-the-round carving, then I also suggest you create this simple bench hook (see

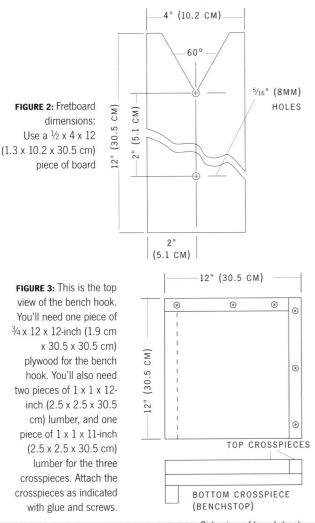

FIGURE 2: Fretboard dimensions: Use a ½ x 4 x 12 (1.3 x 10.2 x 30.5 cm) piece of board

4" (10.2 CM)

60°

⁵⁄₁₆" (8MM) HOLES

12" (30.5 CM)

2" (5.1 CM)

2" (5.1 CM)

FIGURE 3: This is the top view of the bench hook. You'll need one piece of ¾ x 12 x 12-inch (1.9 cm x 30.5 x 30.5 cm) plywood for the bench hook. You'll also need two pieces of 1 x 1 x 12-inch (2.5 x 2.5 x 30.5 cm) lumber, and one piece of 1 x 1 x 11-inch (2.5 x 2.5 x 30.5 cm) lumber for the three crosspieces. Attach the crosspieces as indicated with glue and screws.

12" (30.5 CM)

12" (30.5 CM)

TOP CROSSPIECES

BOTTOM CROSSPIECE (BENCHSTOP)

FIGURE 4: Side view of bench hook

figure 3). The cleat underneath holds the hook in place, while the corner created by the two cleats on the top keeps your carving or blank from sliding away from you as you carve. Clamp the bench hook to your work surface.

Miscellaneous Tools

Electronic woodburning tools can be used to texture, color, and sign your work. If you're using power tools, you'll need dust masks and dust collectors. You'll also need artist tools and brushes when finishing a carving with paint or lacquer. I also suggest using tracing paper and graphite paper for transferring your designs to the wood. A good light source that's color corrected with a magnifying device is great for the eyes when doing fine detail work.

Tool Care

Periodically, you should inspect your tools, wiping them off with an oily rag to guard against rust. Store your tools in individual compartments or in a cloth roll to protect them and reduce your time spent resharpening them.

SHARPENING TOOLS

Always keep your tools sharp, and stop carving every so often to hone them to keep a keen edge. Every carver I know has developed his own system for sharpening; each has found a procedure that works for him, and that's what counts. Some use oil stones, water stones, or man-made stones, and some power sharpen.

The first step is to whet the blade, using a medium- to fine-grit abrasive, such as a diamond hone or emery paper. Push the edge into the hone until you develop a burr or wire edge on the blade. Then turn the blade over and develop the burr on the other side. The next step, using a finer grit, is called honing, and it removes the edge burr and surface roughness produced in the whetting stage. Your final step is to polish the blade and edge to a mirror finish with a polishing compound to further reduce the surface friction between the blade and the wood.

How do you tell if your blade is sharp? Check the sharpness by making a cut across the grain of a piece of scrap wood. If you get a shiny, smooth cut, then the blade's sharp. If the grain tears out, or if the surface is rough or grooved, then you know that you need to hone the edge some more.

Whetting the blade on a diamond stone

SUGGESTED TOOLS

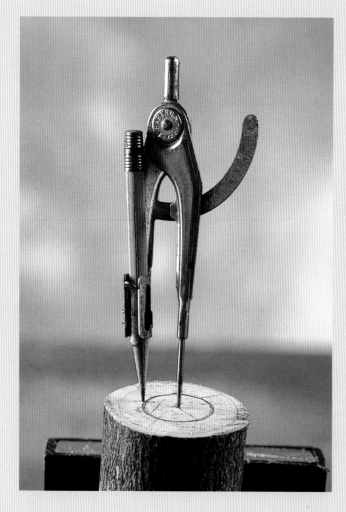

Pencil
Ruler
Compass/dividers
Tracing paper
Graphite paper

Sanding Tools and Materials

Sandpaper (150 to 400 grit)
Cloth-backed abrasives
Open-abrasive screens
Flexible plastic abrasive pads (gray and white)

Holding Devices
(at least one of the following)

Bench hook (see page 10)
C-clamp
Vise
Lag screw
Rubber pad to carve on (router pad)

Finishing Materials

Tack cloth
Wood glue
Penetrating and/or surface finishes, as desired

Safety Equipment

Bandages
Carving glove
Finger guards

As a minimum, you should have the following tools and materials for the carving projects in this book.

Carving Tools

Knife (fixed-blade is recommended)
Four straight gouges (palm gouges will do fine)
#3 sweep gouge, ½ inch (1.3 cm) wide
#7 sweep gouge, ½ inch (1.3 cm) wide
#11 sweep (veiner) gouge, ¼ inch (6 mm) wide
#12 sweep (V-parting) gouge, ¼ inch (6 mm) wide

Drawing Supplies and Pattern-Making Materials

Use of a photocopying machine
Coping saw
Fret board (see page 10)
Drawing supplies

WOOD

The natural beauty and unique qualities of wood allow a carver to transform it with patience and care into a vision of beauty and warmth. You can buy wood, blanks or rough outs for carving from craft and hobby stores or over the Internet. Woodcarving catalogs are also a good source. Of course, you can also make your own blanks. But before purchasing or finding your wood, there are some major factors to consider.

Moisture Content

Freshly cut green wood is easier to carve than the same wood after it has been seasoned or kiln-dried. Green wood is also more susceptible to cracking and splitting as it dries out, unless you take steps to control the drying or relieve the internal stresses. You'll have fewer of these problems using kiln-dried wood for your projects.

Weight or Density

While the moisture content does contribute to the weight in freshly cut green wood, you'll find, in general, that heavier, denser woods are more difficult to carve than lighter woods. In my experience, it usually takes me two to three times longer to carve the same project in walnut as it does to carve it in basswood or sugar pine.

Condition of the Wood

The grain, knots, and other defects, as well as inclusions in "found" wood, can result in serious problems. Nails, barbed wire, bullets, and sand inclusions can damage your tools. A heavy or twisted grain may cause your tools to follow it instead of going where you want them to go, particularly when you're carving against the grain. The key is to always look over your wood closely to avoid difficulties in carving.

Kinds of Wood

There are softwoods, hardwoods, and imported woods to choose from. The availability and cost are important factors to consider. In general, hardwoods are more difficult to carve than softwoods. Wood with a wild grain is harder to carve, but it often produces beautiful, smooth, stylized carvings. A close-grained wood is better when you need fine details. In my opinion, the following woods are the most easily carved in each category:

Imported woods	Softwoods	Hardwoods
Lime *(linden)*	White pine	Basswood *(linden)*
Mahogany *(Honduran)*	Sugar pine	Butternut
Spanish cedar	Ponderosa pine	Buckeye

The fun comes in finding just the right wood for your project, or finding a piece that speaks to you. Several years ago, one of my students had an old pine board with four knots in it. She carved a beautiful relief carving of two owls sitting on a branch. She used the knots as the eyes of the owls. She enjoyed every minute she spent carving her serendipitous piece.

In the event you can't find wood the right size for your project, you can always resort to gluing thinner boards together. You may want to use this technique to build strength into your blank by orienting the grain in a particular direction for a specific area of your carving. In some cases, this will also reduce the amount of waste wood that needs to be removed. The joints are no problem for a painted project. By using different colored woods and carving away the layers, you can obtain other interesting effects.

Finally, if you're new to carving, start with basswood or sugar pine until you acquire some experience. Both woods are relatively easy to carve and hold carved details well.

PATTERNS AND BLANKS

Once you've chosen your wood, the next step is to transfer the pattern or template to the wood. Always begin by marking the horizontal and vertical centerlines on the pattern and the wood. Next, carefully align the two sets of centerlines to check the fit of the pattern to the wood (1). You may want to adjust your location to avoid defects in the wood or to take advantage of the grain, color, or imperfections in the wood.

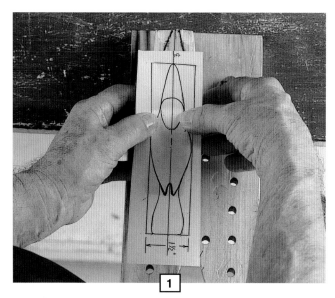

Transferring the Pattern

You can use any of the following methods to transfer the pattern to the wood (2):

- Glue your patterns directly to the wood with rubber cement.
- Tape one edge of your pattern to the wood and place a sheet of graphite paper under your pattern (don't use carbon paper). Then trace the pattern using a colored pencil so that you can be sure you have transferred the complete design.
- Chalk or graphite the back side of your pattern, and rub the front side with a stylus to mark the wood.
- By ironing a photocopy of the pattern onto the wood, you'll obtain a reverse image of your design.
- Scan actual completed carvings on your computer scanner, and use the printed scan as the pattern.

For in-the-round carvings, align the centerlines and transfer both the side profile view and the front or top view to the wood. I usually use graphite paper for this purpose.

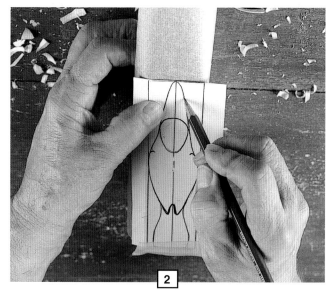

For relief carvings, you need only a single view. It's helpful in relief carving to use a graph system on both your pattern and on the wood so that you can re-establish the design after you've carved away the various levels.

Cutting the Outline (Creating the Blank)

Use the fret board (see page 10) clamped to your work surface to support the wood to help you cut a square edge with a coping saw. Or better yet, use a jigsaw or bandsaw to cut out your blank. Always be sure your wood is square before you start. It's usually best to cut out your side profile first and tape or use rubber cement to reattach the waste wood you've cut off (3). This gives you a square surface for your next cuts. Then cut out the top or front profile. Now mark the centerlines on all four sides of the cutout blank. You're now ready to start carving.

CARVING TECHNIQUES

All the projects in this book can be classified as either in-the-round or relief. In-the-round carving consists of creating a three-dimensional piece, while relief carving is two dimensional. And though both kinds of carving involve different techniques and tools, you'll follow the same four basic steps or phases for both.

During the outlining phase you begin by using the design pattern to cut out your blank or outline your design (if doing relief carving). During the shaping phase, you're removing waste wood to arrive at the basic design shape. During the detailing phase, you use smaller, defined cuts to bring out the details one by one until you're satisfied with the overall appearance. Finally, during the finishing phase, you can leave your project as it is, or decide on the many different kinds of finishes noted on page 23.

In-the-Round Carving

My years of teaching woodcarving have taught me that the best way to learn is by doing. So in order to describe the techniques needed for the in-the-round carving projects in this book, I'll first show you the basic cuts you need to master, and then launch you right into a project that you can't possibly mess up. This learning project is called Ur Bird, and the best thing about this bird is that no two are alike, and there's no right or wrong way to carve it. If you make a mistake or have a problem, don't hesitate to change the design. Have fun, relax, and enjoy this project. You'll not only develop the technical skills needed for the rest of the projects, but also learn the limitations of your tools and materials.

The Cuts to Know

When working on three-dimensional pieces, you'll usually use your knife to make the cuts that gradually shape your design. There are five types of cuts used.

■ The stop cut is probably the most important carving cut of all. It severs the grain so the next cut will slice into it and not damage the design.

■ The slicing cut is a straight pushing cut that slices across the wood fibers, usually removing long curls of wood. Used in combination with the stop cut, you can safely rough out the basic shape.

■ With the paring cut, the blade is pulled towards the thumb of the hand holding the knife, while the thumb steadies the wood. Be sure to keep your thumb out of the way or protect it with a thumb guard, tape, or glove.

■ The rolling and slicing cut is used in curved areas where you need to scoop out the waste wood. As it scoops and rolls in the curve, the blade of the knife also slices across the fibers, producing a smooth surface.

Cutting Tips

■ A lot of cutting is done with the tip of your knife. When you're making tight curves, stand your knife up and use the tip to reduce the amount of drag. Use the tip when you're starting a hole or in detailing. At times, a rocking or sawing action with your knife will be useful.

■ The levering cut is useful in tight areas where close control is required. With the cutting edge facing away from you, use the thumb of the other hand as a fulcrum point on the back of the blade and pivot the knife into the wood by pulling back on the knife handle. You can really nibble the waste wood away with this cut.

■ Carving with the grain is always easier than carving against or across the grain. With experience, you'll learn by feel when you're carving against the grain. When an experienced carver feels this happening, he'll automatically turn his wood 180° so that he's carving with the grain.

■ Another important cut is an undercut. This is used to cast a shadow that produces depth in your carving. It is particularly useful in relief carving. It's an angled stop cut. Your slicing cut that removes the waste wood ends up under the edge of the design.

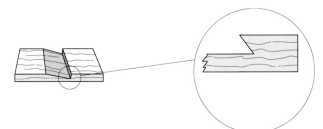

The normal view shows how the slicing cut ends at a stop cut. The exploded view shows what an undercut looks like.

Once you've cut out the basic design, you now have the blank.

The Shaping Phase

As you carve, try not to carve away the centerlines, which you'll use to help you carve symmetrically so you don't end up with a lopsided bird. If you carve the centerline away, redraw it right away. Try to carve out equal amounts of waste wood on either side of the centerlines.

The first cut you make is a stop cut across the tail at the end of the wing (4). Carve away the waste wood on the top of the tail with a slicing cut (5). Because the tail is thin,

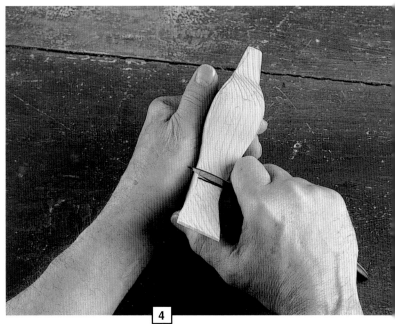

4

UR BIRD

Now that you've got the basic cuts down, it's time to carve! Use basswood or white pine for this project. Examine your wood carefully for flaws, and check the grain direction. Make sure the grain runs lengthwise to the bird. Check the list on page 12 to make sure you have the tools you need.

The Outlining Phase

See page 14 for instructions on marking your centerlines and transferring the pattern to the wood. See page 77 for the patterns.

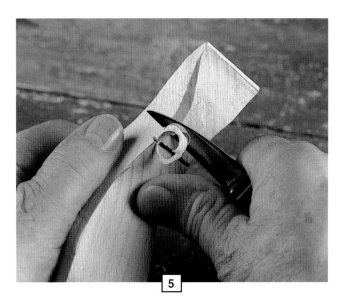

5

use light slicing cuts; and in order to maintain strength, taper the tail to the outer edges, keeping the full thickness along the centerline. The thin edge tricks the eye into thinking the tail is thin. The slicing cut can fool you. As you push the blade through the wood, you must also move it to one side so that it slices the fibers.

Now use this same slicing cut to round over the rest of the blank. Take care to use fairly long, light strokes to begin with. Woodcarver Rick Butz has a saying: "Three small cuts are better than one big cut." So take it easy until you've learned when to make a heavy cut. You'll also find it necessary to use the other basic cuts as you develop the form.

Mark a circle on the top of the bird's head to help as you round off this area using paring cuts (6). A bird's neck

tapers from the head to the body, and there's no distinct necking in, so don't remove too much wood in this area. Now use a series of paring or slicing cuts to taper the beak. Check the grain direction and carefully carve the shape you want. You'll probably find it necessary to use the levering or push cut during this rounding and shaping phase. Work all around your blank and continue to develop the overall shape (7).

Now look at the base. What shape do you want to create? Square, oval, round? Mark the bottom outline to guide your next cuts. This curved area from the body to the base is a difficult area to carve (you're carving across the surface grain in a tight area), requiring the use of the rolling and slicing cut. As you make your cut, roll the blade in a scooping action, and try not to force your blade straight through the wood. This will result in a tear out of the grain.

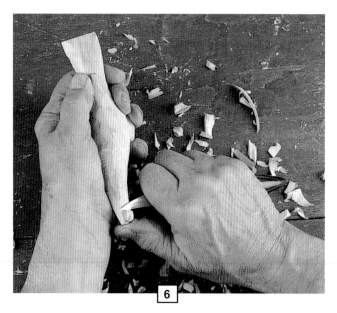

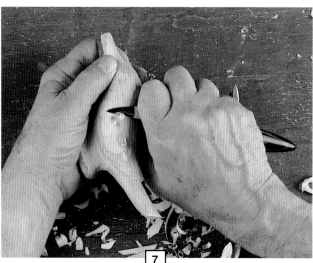

Try to make it slice across the grain at the same time you roll it (8). This will result in a smooth surface rather than a rough area of pulled-out fibers.

The Detailing Phase

Having developed the basic shape you want, you can now begin to detail your bird. Use a pencil to establish the wing lines and the eye positions. Use a narrow strip of paper folded in half to make sure the eyes are level. Align the fold with your top centerline, with the strip draping over both sides. Mark the eye position on one side through the paper, and remove the paper strip. Fold it in half as before, now mark through the paper so that the eye position is the same distance from the fold (9). Align the fold with the centerline again, and mark the eye position on the other side of the bird. The same technique can be used to draw in the wing lines.

Stop cut along the wing line from the breast to the tail (10). Don't cut too deeply. Now undercut from below into the stop cut. Reshape the area under the wing. You may also want to carve some feathers in the wing and in the tail (11). Use an eye tool, nail set, or awl to form the eyes (12).

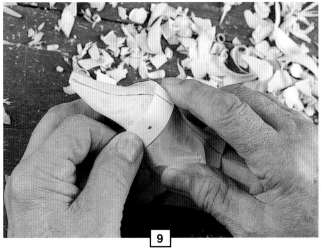

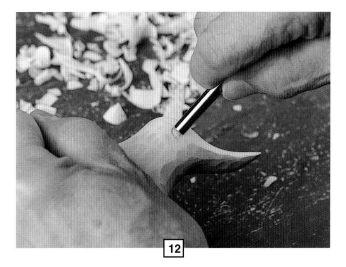

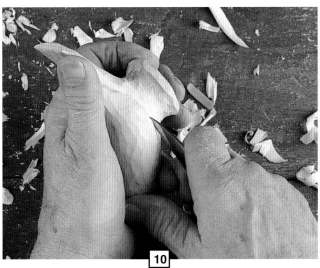

The Finishing Phase

Use the information on pages 21 to 23 to finish your bird, or leave it as it is. You can do as little or as much as you want in the way of detailing, but remember that simple is usually better than too much. Don't forget to sign and date your masterpiece.

RELIEF CARVING

There are basically four types of relief carving. The simplest is incised carving, which is a lot like engraving. Usually the relief carving you see is low relief and is relatively shallow. The coins in your pocket are an example of low relief. When more than half the thickness of the wood is removed, it's called high relief or deep-relief carving. Reverse relief is where the design is carved into the background. Butter or cookie molds are carved this way. Half round and pierced carvings are usually considered versions of relief carvings. When first trying relief carving, select relatively simple designs. Avoid intricate shapes and heavy undercutting.

The value of shadows and the effect of lighting is very important in bringing out the beauty of the design. From time to time as you're carving, step back and hold up your carving to check the effect of light and shadows. To create the illusion of depth, you must follow the rules

Relief Carving: Four Stages

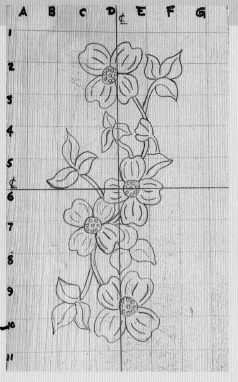

The suggested way to transfer a pattern for relief carving

A relief-carved piece during the outlining phase (notice the rounded corners—try to avoid square corners)

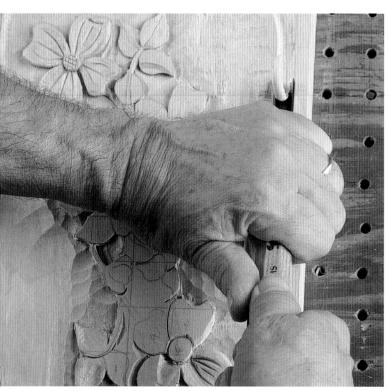

Establishing the border outline with a gouge

of perspective. Objects in the background must be smaller in size. All lines that are parallel will eventually narrow to a vanishing point. Check drawing books for a more complete explanation of these principles of perspective.

Using Gouges

Though you can use a knife for many steps, gouges will often make life easier for you. When using a gouge, hold its handle in your right hand (if you're right-handed), with your thumb pointing toward the cutting edge. Your left hand should grasp the blade with the thumb pointing toward the handle. Push with your right hand, or use a mallet to make your cut. Your left hand guides the tool or holds back to control the cut. You can also use the palm of the right hand to push the gouge. Stand erect and avoid stooping over to reduce overtiring and/or a backache. When using a mallet, snap your wrist and let the mallet do the work.

A similar carving with a rounded outline during the shaping phase

A completed carving with a more natural-looking border

SANDING AND FINISHING

When you lay down your knife and gouges, thinking that you're done, you'll find that you're actually only halfway through. Now the sanding and finishing stage starts.

Take a good look at your carving. Hold it up to the light. How does the light affect its overall appearance? Do the shadows enhance the design? What shading or color do you want to use? Is the surface texture right? Do you want the "as carved" look, or do you think a sleek, smooth overall appearance would be better? What type of finish do you need to protect and seal the wood satisfactorily? However you answer these questions, the important thing to remember is that a poor finish or bad color combination can ruin even the best carving.

Sanding

If you want a really smooth finish, sanding is vital. I like to use an open abrasive rather than fiber-backed abrasives, because they do not load up, and I can vary the width of

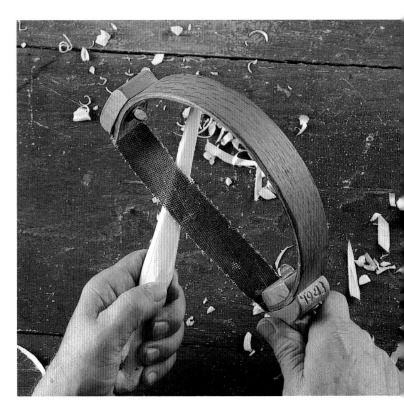

Flexible sander with open abrasive

the abrasive in a flexible holder to suit the carving. Experiment with different abrasives until you find the ones that work best for you.

Most abrasive sheets are graded from coarse to very fine. The coarse abrasives (60 to 100 grit) can be used to actually remove as much wood as you could using a knife. Some carvers use them for roughing out to get the basic shape. Use 120- to 180-grit abrasives for initial smoothing and 200- to 600-grit abrasives for final smoothing.

SANDING YOUR CARVING

Most of your sanding should be done with the grain. Always keep moving your abrasive so you don't cause grooves or flat spots in the wood. Don't push too hard; let the abrasive do the work. Be aware that you can actually burn the wood with a power sander. Also, breathing in too much wood dust can be dangerous, so use a dust collector or wear a face mask.

Use a sponge or spray to moisten (don't soak) the wood with water or a 50/50 solution of water and alcohol to raise the wood grain. When the wood dries, sand off the fuzz with a 320- to 400-grit abrasive or a plastic abrasive pad. This will lessen the amount of fuzz when you apply a sanding sealer.

Let your carving set for 24 hours or longer and then sand it again. Any changes in the humidity will also raise the fuzz. By waiting and sanding a second time you'll get a smoother finish. A sanding sealer will also raise the grain, requiring additional sanding for that really smooth finish.

Finishing

The purpose of a finish is to protect the wood, and selection of a finish is a matter of choice. Any finish will change the color of the wood to some degree, so experiment on a scrap of wood first. Or, better yet, prepare different wood samples with different finishes as a reference.

SURFACE FILM FINISHES

Surface film finishes penetrate the wood surface only slightly, with each coat building upon the previous one. Among them are varnish, shellac, lacquer, clear plastic, and polyurethane finishes. Some of these products have a nitrocellulose base and are highly flammable and toxic. Even mineral-base finishes are unpleasant to use without good ventilation. All finishes can be brushed, sprayed, or dipped on. You can also use a sanding sealer, which has a filler in it that fills the pores and grain, to produce a level base for a final finish.

APPLYING SURFACE FILM FINISHES

Regardless of the resin type or kind of solvent, a beautiful, smooth finish can be obtained by following the manufacturer's directions. Good adhesion of the sealer coat (first coat) is important, and the higher the humidity, the more difficult it is to apply. Several thin coats are better than one heavy coat, and it's critical that each coat is completely dry before the next coat is applied. The first coat raises the grain. After this coat is completely dry, sand it back. Use a tack cloth to remove sanding dust, and apply the second coat. When cured, sand it back again, and apply the final coat. You can easily rub through the finish, so go easy and use very fine abrasives, or you may have to start over again to get the final finish the way you want it.

An old reliable finish is beeswax. Use a double boiler and melt the beeswax, then add boiled linseed oil (about half and half). Use a soft cloth and rub it in by hand. This gives your carving a protective coating that can be renewed easily anytime.

When applying a lacquer finish, I often make my carving of a size so that I can dip it directly in the can and get a heavier coat. A rule of thumb is that one dip coat is equal to two or three brush coats, and one brush coat is the equivalent of two or three spray coats.

PENETRATING FINISHES

Among the penetrating oil finishes are tung, linseed, and Danish oils. Danish oils are a mixture of oil and varnish. Both tung oil and linseed oil come raw and boiled (refined). Use the boiled varieties (or you'll be waiting an eternity for the raw oil finish to dry), and rub them in by hand. Apply as many coats as you like—the more coats, the more protection.

APPLYING PENETRATING FINISHES

With oil finishes, your wood must be clean, sanded or scraped, and wiped clean with a tack cloth. Then flood the surface with oil and rub off the excess. Wipe off the oil completely to obtain a hand-rubbed look. How long you let it dry depends on the humidity, though usually

24 hours is enough. Watch for bleed back—excess oil that seeps out of the wood. The pores of the wood are usually sealed after two coats. The important thing to remember with oil finishes is that you're applying thin coats. Be patient; the subsequent coats will produce the finish and protection you want. The buildup of coats will last for years, though leaving too much oil on the wood surface or re-coating before the previous coat is dry can cause problems.

Caution: Dispose of your oily rags carefully, and let them dry outdoors. They can burst into flames under the right conditions. Keep them in a covered metal container until you dispose of them.

Surface Finishes

■ Finished surface texture treatments include any or all of the following: As carved, as sanded, stamped or tooled, burned, roughened or distressed, and sand-blasted.

■ Surface color treatments include natural, clear (lacquer varnish), oil, plastic, wax, watercolor paints, oil paints, acrylic paints, gilding, airbrush techniques, and liquid shoe polish.

■ For surface durability, use sealer coats, vegetable or nut oil finish (for carved food utensils), super glue (to harden thin fragile areas), polyurethane coatings (for a high, hard gloss), and/or wax.

■ For special effects, you can add metal feet or glass eyes for animals and birds, wood veneer for feathers, jeweler's findings, buckles, and/or pipe stems.

Mounts and Bases

Your finishing touch should be a base, frame, or mount that complements your carving. The base can easily make or break your carving's appearance. It should always provide a stable, secure mounting; think of the base as the bottom of a triangle. It may be an integral part of your carving, or it may be a simple frame around a relief carving. It should not overpower your carving. For a realistic animal or bird carving, select your habitat, twigs, rocks, leaves, etc., carefully. A finished walnut or mahogany base can be purchased from one of the carving supply houses.

You can use simple wooden blocks of varying size and color grouped appropriately to unite individual carvings. A simple shelf with a spotlight will really show off your carving. Experiment first with different arrangements before you select your final mounting for your masterpiece.

SAFETY

Most accidents can be prevented with a little common sense. We all assume nothing bad is going to happen, but accidents usually occur when we're tired or when we hurry. Here are some safety tips to consider before starting:

■ Have bandages and a first-aid kit close at hand. Direct pressure with a gauze pad is the best immediate treatment for cuts.
■ Maintain good working conditions. Have a place for everything and keep everything in its place. Provide good light and ventilation.
■ Wear protective equipment, such as gloves, finger guards, dust masks, and goggles, when appropriate.
■ Use properly grounded electrical equipment.
■ Clamp or securely fasten your work, or hold your carving so you avoid carving toward your body.
■ Check which way the grain runs, and carve with the grain as much as possible.
■ Keep your tools sharp.
■ Remember, three small cuts are better than one large cut that can slip and either damage your project or your body.
■ Don't wear loose clothing around rotating power equipment.
■ Keep flammable liquids and oil-soaked rags properly stored. Airborne fumes and wood dust can be explosive and are usually toxic.
■ Molds and fungi reside in some wood and are released into the air when sanded. Respiratory ailments are common in the woodworking industry. Redwood dust, for example, can cause an acute illness that resembles pneumonia. Some exotic woods will produce skin irritations and glandular swelling. Many skin irritations are caused by contact with adhesives and solvents. Epoxies can cause blistering and scaling.
■ Relax and enjoy your carving experience. Practice patience and it will pay off in the quality of your projects.

IDEAS AND DESIGNS

When first starting out, most carvers copy or use the design of another carver or artist to guide their efforts. It's always good to have a model to follow, but the real fun starts when you get the urge to create your own designs. Creating a good carving begins with inspiration. Before the birth of an idea, you should begin a collection of information and pictures on various subjects you find interesting. Clip pictures from newspapers, magazines, greeting cards, and cartoons, and create a filing system for easy retrieval when needed. Being artistic helps; however, there are many books available on the principles of design and proportion.

Carver Rick Butz says, "The success of any carving depends on its visual elements working together." The following steps will help you accomplish this:

■ Observe. When we look at something, we don't always see what we're looking at—many facets may go unnoticed.

■ Research your subject thoroughly, and make sketches of your ideas.

■ Make more sketches of different poses and arrangements. Try to get the basic outline first, then the proper relationship of the parts, or proportion, before you begin to sketch in the details.

■ Work out the problems on paper first, and choose the carving style you like best.

■ Select the sketch that best expresses your ideas.

■ Develop your final design.

Your Final Design

When you have your final design arrangement, use all the modern technology available—computer, scanner, copy machine, etc.—to develop, manipulate, and change the size of your design to fit the wood you've selected.

You may want to make a simple clay model of your design, so you can work out some of the difficult areas and minimize the carving problems. Even a rough clay model will give you a better feel for your portrayal and proportions of your subject. Many carvers use a point-to-point system to transfer measurements from the clay to the wood to aid them in carving. You can use a strong light source and your clay model to make a silhouette outline pattern for cutting out your carving blank.

Roy K. Pace, *Banjo Picker*, 2000. Basswood, watercolors, shellac sealer; knives; 10 ¼ x 3 ½ x 3 in. (26 x 8.9 x 7.6 cm). Photo by artist

Jan Oegema, *London Night Watch*, 1999. Basswood, pine stain, antique wax; hand tools; 30 in. tall. (76.2 cm). Photo by Mike Larmer

Jan Oegema, *Brother & Sis,* 2000. Basswood, acrylic paint, antique finish; band saw, hand tools; 18 x 16 in. (45.7 x 40.6 cm). Photo by Mike Larmer

Jan Oegema, untitled, 2000. Basswood plate, finishing spray; chipcarved; 15 in. (38 cm). Photo by Mike Larmer

Gail Stanek, *Northern Cardinal*, 2000. Tupelo wood, acrylic paints, glass eyes, brass, epoxy; 13 x 9 x 8 in. (33 x 22.9 x 20.3 cm) Photo by artist

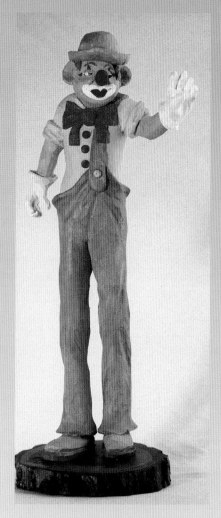

Gail Stanek, *Saw-Whet Owl*, 1997. Tupelo wood, acrylic paints, glass eyes; 8 x 4 x 4 in. (20.3 x 10.2 x 10.2 cm). Photo by artist

Ol' Don Burgdorf, *Tree Top,* 2001. Basswood, acrylic paints, satin polyurethane; 12 x 5 x 2 in. (30.5 x 12.7 x 5 cm). Photo by artist

Gail Stanek, *Eastern Bluebird*, 2001. Tupelo wood, acrylic paints, glass eyes, brass, epoxy; 14 x 8 x 7 in. (35.6 x 20.3 x 17.8 cm). Photo by artist

David Maggard, *Old World Santa.* Basswood; mallet, gouges; 9 in. (22.9 cm) Photo by Tim Barnwell

Desiree Hajny, *Quality Time*, 1998. Butternut; hand tools, woodburner; 4 x 12 x 4 in. (10.2 x 30.5 x 10.2 cm).

Jan Oegema, *Innocence,* 1998. Basswood, bleached and antiqued finish; bandsaw, hand tools; 36 in. tall (91.4 cm). Photo by Mike Larmer

Desiree Hajny, *Grassland Stripes,* 1999. White walnut; hand tools, woodburner; 14 x 10 x 14 in. (35.6 x 25 x 35 cm).

Robert G. Foulkes, *Bjorn,* 1993. Butternut; knife, palm gouges, in-the-round; 6 1/2 x 5 x 4 1/2 in. (16.5 x 12.7 x 11.4 cm). Photo by Lindsay Dixon

Drew Langsner, *Salad Bowl and Serving Spoon,* 2000. Tulip poplar bowl, 5 x 9 x 16 (12.7 x 22.9 x 40.6 cm); yellow birch spoon, 2 x 3 x 14 in. (5 x 7.6 x 35.6 cm). Photo by artist

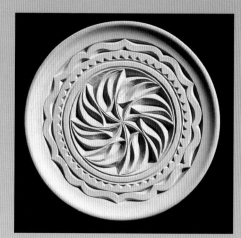

Wayne Barton, *Scalloped Rim Plate,* 1998. Basswood, chip-carving knives; 12 in. (30.5 cm). Photo by artist

Wayne Barton, *Scoop Plate,* 1998. Basswood, chip-carving knives; 6 in. (15.2 cm). Photo by artist

Wayne Barton, *Jewelry Box (lid),* 1997. Butternut, chip-carving knives; 8½ x 14½ (21.6 x 36.8 cm). Photo by artist

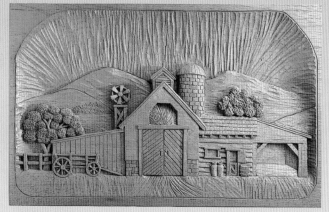

John Hillyer, *Country Barn Scene.* Spanish cedar, knife and gouges; 24 x 15 x 1¾ in. (61 x 38.1 x 4.4 cm). Photo by Sandra Stambaugh

Alice Strom, *Lady of Liberty,* 1999. Basswood, acrylic paint; 23 x 19 x 2½ in. (58.4 x 48.3 x 6.4 cm). Photo by artist

Jan Oegema, *Wild Boar,* 1996. Basswood, oak stain, antique finish; hand tools; 12 x 8 x 6 in. (30.5 x 20.3 x 5 cm). Photo by Mike Larmer

Ted Nichols, *Noah's Ark,* 1992. Basswood, acrylic paint, hand-rubbed finish; ark is 12 x 16 x ½ in. (30.5 x 40.6 x 1.3 cm). Photo by artist

John Hillyer, *Born to Howl.* Basswood, knife and gouges; 8 x 3½ x 3½ in. (20.3 x 8.9 x 8.9 cm). Photo by Sandra Stambaugh

Alice Strom, *Northwoods Moose,* 1999. Basswood, acrylic paint; 9 x 10 in. (22.9 x 25.4 cm).

Nicholas Herrera, *Sacred Heart*, 1998. Wood, watercolors; 22½ x 17½ in. (57.2 x 44.5 cm) Courtesy of Cavin-Morris Inc., New York, New York

Ron Ramsey, *Blue Jay Doors,* 1987. Built-up mahogany, handcarving tools; 84 x 72 x 6 in. (213 x 183 x 15.2 cm). Photo by artist

Ron Ramsey, *Honey Bear Doors*, 1998. Built-up cedar, 80 x 72 x 6 in. (203 x 183 x 15.2 cm). Photo by artist

Trout Key Chain

Here's a great gift for that fisherman in your life who's so hard to buy for.
You could also carve several trout and create a miniature mobile.

YOU WILL NEED
Cedar, walnut, or teak, ½ x 1½ x 4 inches (1.3 x 3.8 x 10.2 cm)
Fixed-blade carving knife
Cloth-backed abrasive, sandpaper, or open abrasive (180 to 220 grit)
Desired finish
Brass screw eye (small)
Drill
Brass key chain and split ring

1 Transfer the patterns on page 78 to a squared piece of wood, and cut your blank. The grain of the wood should run the length of the fish. Make a saw cut for the mouth. Carefully consider the grain and develop a long "S" curve to portray a swimming action before carving. Mark the position of the side fins so you don't carve them off while shaping the fish. Use a combination of long slicing cuts and paring cuts with your knife to develop the "S" shape of the body.

2 Using the template as a guide, locate and draw the gills and side fins. Stop cut the gills and undercut to make them stand out more.

3 Stop cut and undercut the side fins that you drew in step 2.

4 With the knife, develop the shape of the head with levered or paring cuts.

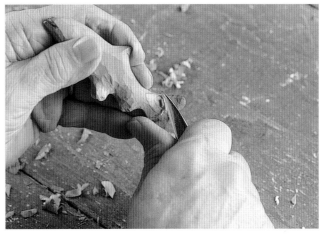

5 Carve a curve into the tail with a paring cut. Make it wavy but not too thin.

6 Carve the wood out from between the two lower pelvic fins. Remember, this is a key chain, so don't make your edges too thin and fragile. Sand the trout smooth with 180- to 220-grit abrasive. Finish as desired. This trout was given three coats of spray lacquer. Install the small brass screw eye in the mouth. To avoid splitting, you may want to drill a pilot hole first. Use the brass chain with a split ring for the keys.

Weed Pot

Making something out of nothing can be a great source of satisfaction. This weed pot, which can be made from a found piece of driftwood, an old beam, or a limb, utilizes a technique called incised carving.

YOU WILL NEED

Driftwood, a tree limb, or found wood, 3 inches (7.6 cm) in diameter, 3 inches (7.6 cm) long

Vise

Compass

Drill, with ¼ inch (6 mm) bit

Fixed-blade carving knife

Draw knife (optional)

Power sander (optional)

#11 veiner carving gouge, ¼-inch (6 mm) wide

Drum sander (optional)

#3 carving gouge, ½ inch (1.3 cm) wide

V-tool gouge, ¼ inch (6 mm) wide

Desired finish

1 Decide on the basic shape of your weed pot, and use the patterns on page 78. Use them as is, or change them to suit your piece. If you want it to be rustic, leave the bark on and carve your design through the bark. The grain of the wood should run vertically. Outline the shape of your design and use a centerline guide. Place the wood in the vise, and use the compass to draw circles of appropriate size on the top and bottom of the wood.

2 Drill a hole through the top about ¼ inch (6 mm) in diameter and about 1½ inches (3.8 cm) deep. This may also help to prevent splitting or cracking of green wood. If you want to use a glass vial in the pot, adjust the size of the hole and the neck diameter accordingly. Use the knife or the draw knife to remove the bark and waste wood.

3 Use the knife or power sander to shape the bottom edge to your satisfaction. If using the knife, you'll most likely be using slicing or paring cuts.

4 With the #11 gouge or a drum sander, carve out the neck. Draw a centerline to help you keep the shape symmetrical and in line with the pot's top and bottom.

5 Once you're happy with the shape of the pot, use the #3 gouge to flatten the front to provide a surface for the inscribed design.

6 The only detail in this project is the incised star. This can be added with the knife or the V-tool. Keep it simple and use shallow cuts.

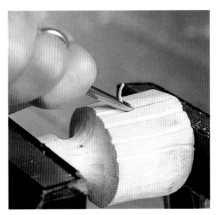

7 Add grooves to the sides using the #11 gouge. Sand or finish to your satisfaction. This finished piece was brushed with two coats of boiled linseed oil. If you've used green wood, you'll probably encounter some splitting or checking. Don't be discouraged if this happens; it adds to the charm of a found-wood article.

Inscribed Plate

A simple incised pattern or chip carving on a basswood plate makes a wonderful wall hanging. Basswood plates of different shapes and sizes are readily available at most carving suppliers, but cherry or walnut plates will probably need to be specially ordered or turned on a lathe for you. You can create incised patterns for almost any object, producing handcrafted items such as stools, tables, plaques, lamp bases, etc.

8-inch (20.3 cm) basswood plate or turned plate

Bench hook, clamped to work surface

Fixed-blade carving knife

V-tool gouge, ¼ inch (6 mm) wide (optional)

Cloth-backed abrasive, sandpaper, or open abrasive (220 or 320 grit)

Mineral, walnut, or vegetable oil (optional)

Desired finish

1 Transfer the pattern on page 78 to the plate. Make sure you align the leaves in the pattern with the grain to minimize cross-grain cuts. Place the plate in the clamped bench hook, and use the knife to carve your cross-grain cuts first. Use the tip of your knife to go around tight corners. Try to visualize where the tip of your knife is going next. For good control, it's important to grip the knife close to the blade and to keep your thumb and knuckles of the carving hand in contact with the wood as you carve.

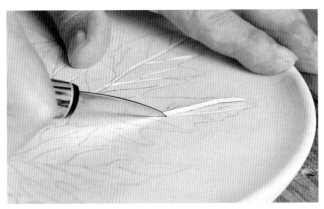

2 When outlining with the knife, make sure you don't cut too deeply. About ¹⁄₁₆ inch (2 mm) is deep enough. Each line of the design will be cut twice by the knife. The first knife cut is a stop cut, followed by a sloping cut to form the V-groove. Turn your wood as you carve.

3 Some carvers prefer to use a V-tool to incise their design, since they only have to make one cut instead of the two they have to make with the knife. Using the V-tool is very much like engraving, and a light touch is needed. Start with your cross-grain cuts first.

4 Continue carving with the V-tool, and use care in the tight corners. Once you're finished carving (either with the knife or V-tool), erase all pencil and carbon marks. Sand very lightly with 220- or 320-grit abrasive in order to maintain the crispness of your cuts. Finish as desired. This project was finished with three coats of spray lacquer. An alternate finish that provides color is done by staining or painting your plate first and then carving through to expose the clear wood. A mineral, walnut, or vegetable oil finish should be used if you intend to use your plate with food.

Letter Opener

Woodcarving is not just a way to create wood chips or to amuse yourself, but a way of producing useful, beautiful objects from a piece of wood. You really only need a knife and some sandpaper for this project, but the other tools and materials listed simplify matters some.

YOU WILL NEED
Basswood or white pine, 1¼ x 1¼ x 9 inches (3.2 x 3.2 x 22.9 cm)
Drill, with a ³⁄₁₆-inch (5 mm) bit
Fixed-blade carving knife
#11 veiner gouge, ¼ inch (6 mm) wide (optional)
Awl
Flexible sander or other sanding device
Desired finish

1 Transfer the patterns on page 78 to a squared piece of wood and cut your blank. The grain of the wood should run the length of the letter opener. Mark and drill a 3/16-inch (5 mm) hole under the duck's neck (as shown on the template). To start shaping, use long slicing cuts with the knife forming the tapered blade. Leave the bottom of the opener flat.

2 Carefully round over and carve away the waste wood around the duck with the knife, using slicing and paring cuts as you go.

3 Enlarge the hole under the neck using the tip of your knife. Carve the neck and head areas using slicing and paring cuts.

4 When detailing the head, make sure the eyes are on the same line (see pages 18 to 19 for one way to do this), and groove out the eye sockets with the knife or #11 gouge. Double-check the symmetry, then use the awl to form the eyes.

5 Sketch in the wings and the split at the tail. Stop cut the wings, and round the body into the stop cut. Notch the wings above the tail. Lightly groove the bill.

6 You can use the flexible sander or other sanding device to smooth the surface. Finish as desired. This piece was finished with three coats of lacquer.

Stretching Cat

The stretching cat on a block started out as just a cat that sat on the edge of a shelf. Unfortunately, vibrations from an 18-wheeler or a rambunctious child are usually enough to cause the cat to move off the shelf and fall to the floor, where it may end up with a broken tail or paw. As a result, I mounted the cat on a block, and now it stays put.

YOU WILL NEED

Basswood, walnut, cherry, or wood of your choice, 1½ x 3½ x 5¼ inches (3.8 x 8.9 x 13.3 cm)

Fixed-blade carving knife

Backsaw

Flexible sander

Riffler file

Cloth-backed abrasive, sandpaper, or open abrasive (150 to 320 grit)

Desired finish

Wood glue or double-sided adhesive tape

Wood block, 2 x 2 x 3 inches (5.1 x 5.1 x 7.6 cm)

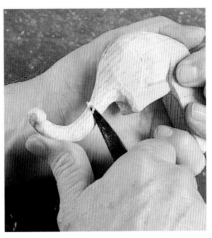

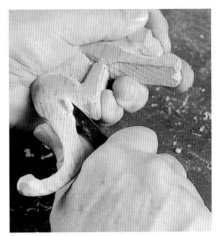

1 Transfer the patterns on page 78 to a squared piece of wood, and cut your blank. The grain of the wood should run the length of the tail. You may want to leave a little extra stock on the tail for sturdiness during the initial carving. Using the knife, carve between the ears and develop the shape of the head. As you carve the head, point the ears slightly. Keep the top of the nose flat. Use a rolling cut to form the eye sockets about halfway from the tip of the nose to the ears.

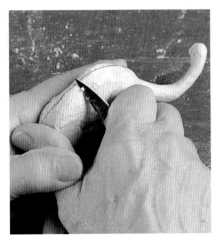

2 Use the knife to round over the body from the centerline. Work all over, and don't concentrate on any one spot too long. Try to leave your centerlines until you're ready to sand. Don't remove the wood between the legs at this stage or carve too much off the tail.

3 Carve the tail using paring and slicing cuts. Make sure to give the tail some curvature for action. Don't make it too thin.

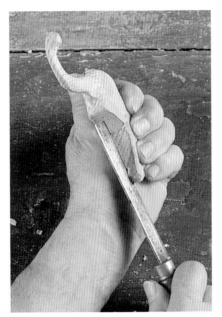

4 Saw a slit between the legs with the backsaw, and mark the outline of the bottom of the paws as a guide for how much to take off when carving the legs.

5 Carve the paws first and then the legs, tapering them from the paws to the body. Also round the front edges of the legs and taper them to the underside slightly. Don't make the legs too thin.

6 Little or no detailing is required in a stylized carving, since the beauty comes from the slick smooth shape. Using the flexible sander will make getting a smooth, curved surface easier. Use the riffler file or a strip of abrasive (150 grit) to smooth between the legs. Smooth out the knife cuts using 180-grit abrasive strips. When you're satisfied with the overall shape and smoothness, go back over the whole cat again with 220-grit abrasive, removing any 180-grit marks. You may have to repeat the procedure with 320-grit abrasive to get the final smoothness you want. Finish as desired. Use either glue or double-sided tape to attach the cat to its block.

Scotty Dog

As a boy, years ago, I saw woodcarvings of miniature Scotty dogs. The sharp cuts made them look so realistic. Some years later, I carved a full-sized Scotty that acts as a doorstop in our house. This project is small enough to carry in your pocket and carve wherever, and whenever, time permits.

YOU WILL NEED

Basswood or white pine, ¾ x 2 x 3¼ inches (1.9 x 5.1 x 8.2 cm)

Fixed-blade carving knife

70° V-tool gouge, ¼ inch (6 mm) wide (optional)

Awl or nail set (optional)

Desired finish

1 Transfer the patterns on page 78 to a squared piece of wood, and cut your blank with the grain running in the vertical direction. With the knife, make a stop cut at the eyebrows on each side of the nose to form a flat surface for the eyes and the sides of the nose. Use a slicing cut on each side of the nose up to your stop cut. This should form the flat sides of the nose.

2 Use the knife to stop cut under the front legs and over the hips of the hind legs.

3 Round over the back and belly areas into the stop cuts you just created.

4 Carve the notch between the ears, and slope the outsides. Remove a V-cut on either side behind the eyebrows with the knife or V-tool. Make another V-cut along the lower jaw, forming the neck and shoulder area.

5 Carefully remove the waste wood between the legs in front.

6 Create a small groove around the tip of the nose with the knife.

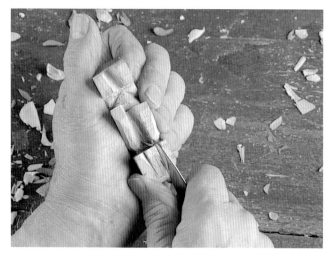

7 Make two V-cuts below the nose to form the chin and the whiskers. Use the knife, awl, or nail set to form the eyes. You can also use a couple of black map pins for the eyes.

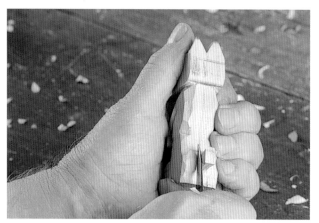

8 Remove the waste wood from both sides of the tail, and add V-cuts to make the tail look shaggy.

9 Use the point of the knife to take out a triangular chip for the mouth. Use the same technique to hollow out the ears. In order to give the dog a shaggy coat, you'll need to make a number of sharp notches or V-cuts. You can use either the knife or the V-tool. Break up the flat surfaces on the sides of the legs, tail, and jaw with these cuts. Not much sanding is needed. Finish as desired.

Miniature Mask

Originally, mask-making was a tribal custom. Usually the witch doctor or shaman carved masks for ceremonial dances or to scare away evil spirits. This mask is a miniature, but you can make it any size you want by enlarging the template with a photocopy machine or computer scanner. A series of mounted and framed miniature masks makes an impressive display.

YOU WILL NEED

Sassafras, catalpa, paulownia, or butternut, 1½ x 3¼ x 7 inches (3.8 x 8.2 x 17.8 cm)

Bench hook, clamped to work surface

Fixed-blade carving knife

Assorted gouges or draw knife (optional)

#11 veiner gouge, ½ inch (1.3 cm) wide

Drill, with ½-inch (1.3 cm) bit (optional)

Cloth-backed abrasive, sandpaper, or open abrasive (150 to 220 grit)

Desired finish

1 Transfer the patterns on page 79 to a squared piece of wood, and cut your blank. The grain of the wood should run the length of the face. Place the blank in the bench hook and use the knife, along with gouges and/or the draw knife, to develop the overall shape. Make sure the general shape is tapered and rounded appropriately.

2 Redraw the pattern as necessary on the rounded surface, and use the #11 gouge to establish the eyebrows. Make your cross-grain cuts first, particularly under the eyebrows and around the mouth. Use the #11 gouge to form the mounds for the eyes.

3 Use the #11 gouge to establish the mouth and chin.

4 With the same gouge, carefully carve out the inside of the mouth. You can also use a drill with a ½-inch (1.3 cm) bit. Don't stop cut these areas. The veiner will leave a smooth curve and reduce the sanding needed. Hold your mask up periodically to check your progress. Is it symmetrical? Is the shape right? Is it smooth enough at this stage?

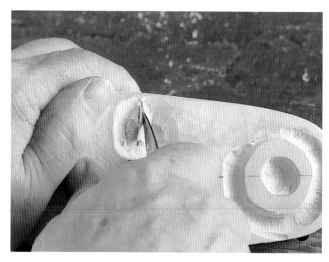

5 Re-mark the eye slits on the eye mounds, and use the knife to carve the slits. They don't have to go any deeper than ⅜ inch (1 cm). Also, don't make them too wide. Use 150- to 220-grit abrasive to sand the surface smooth and remove your knife marks. Keep the edges of the eyebrows and nose sharp. Finish as desired. This project was sprayed with three coats of lacquer. You may want to add a coat of paste wax for a dull sheen.

Love Spoon

Utensils carved from wood are called "treenware." Hand-carved spoons have been produced for centuries in Scandinavian countries. In England, the Welsh "love spoons" have a long tradition—to show his devotion, a young Welshman carves his lady love an elaborate spoon. This project has a Celtic knot in the handle, and if you want, you may omit the ring.

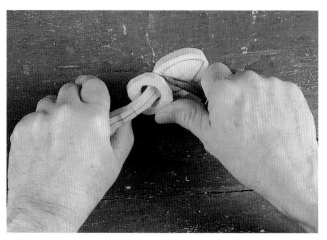

2 Redraw the pattern, and saw out the top view. Then, with the knife, carefully carve enough waste wood to free the ring so that you can move it out of the way.

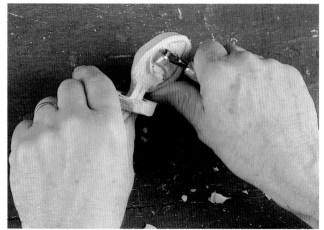

3 Mark a line ⅛ inch (3 mm) inside the edge of the spoon's bowl as a guideline. Carve out the inside of the spoon's bowl using the scorp, #7 gouge, or curved knife. Carve the cross-grain areas first, and hollow the bowl about ⅜ inch (1 cm) deep.

1 Transfer the patterns on page 78 to a squared piece of wood, and cut your blank. The grain of the wood should run the vertical length of the spoon. Mark and drill the five ⅛-inch (3 mm) holes in the handle that are indicated on the pattern. With the saw, remove the waste areas shown on the side view of the pattern.

4 Carve the outside of the bowl using the knife or flexible sander. Sand the inside and outside

smooth with 150-grit abrasive. Round or taper the handle from the centerline to the outside edges with the knife. Form the area for the surface design.

7 Shape the ring into a circular form with the knife, and smooth the finished surface. Use 220- to 320-grit abrasive to produce a really smooth surface finish on the spoon and ring.

5 Carefully sketch the knot so that you're sure you know which strand goes over and which strand goes under the other. Using your knife or V-tool, begin carving the outline of the strands.

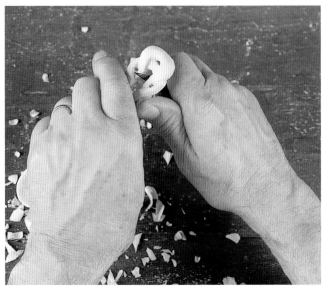

6 Keep the knots as thick as possible. Cut each to the same depth, and continue carving until you have the complete knot smoothly rounded.

8 A simple Nordic decorative treatment called "Kolrosing" can add interest to your spoon. Use the tip of your knife to lightly inscribe a design on the handle. Rub the black walnut dust or instant coffee into the lines. Sand very lightly with 320-grit abrasive, and burnish the design with the handle of your knife. When you apply an oil finish, the design will stand out darker and crisper. The mineral, walnut, or salad oil finish should be used if you intend to use the spoon with food.

Roly-Poly Santa

There are countless carved versions of Santa available from all over the world. This guy's a great fall weekend project—when the chill of winter keeps you indoors and the smell of white pine wood chips fills the air. So, pick up your knife and a block of wood, relax, and fall under Santa's spell.

White pine or basswood, 1½ x 1½ x 4 inches (3.8 x 3.8 x 10.2 cm) or a large basswood goose egg

Fixed-blade carving knife

70° V-tool gouge, ¼ inch (6 mm) wide

#3 gouge, ¼ inch (6 mm) wide

Desired finish

1 Transfer the patterns on page 79 to a squared piece of wood, and cut your blank. The grain of the wood should run the vertical length of the piece. Mark the ear positions so you won't carve them away when you're shaping the carving. With the knife, round over the corner edges and develop the rounded egg shape with a flat bottom. Sketch the basic positions of the hat with the ball on the end. Use care not to cut the ball off in the shaping phase.

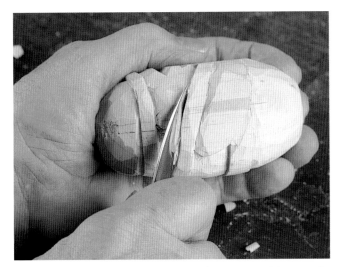

2 Sketch the fur trim on his jacket. Locate his arms and mittens. With the knife, stop cut the collar and the fur trim at the bottom of the jacket, as well as the cuffs. Stop cut the arms and mittens. Use the knife to round over the arms, cuffs, and mittens.

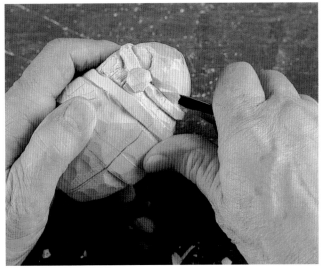

3 With the knife, use paring cuts to carve the trim and ball of the hat. This area is cross-grain, so use care, and don't apply too much pressure or pry with the knife.

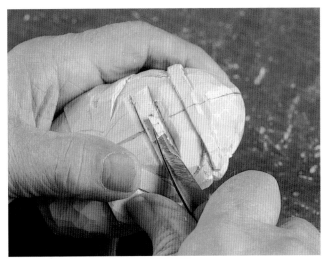

4 The face is always a challenge. Every carver does it just a little differently, and once you have more experience, you'll develop your own method. Draw a horizontal line across the face area about ⅜ inch (1 cm) below the bottom of the cap, and stop cut along the line about ⅛ inch (3 mm) deep. Draw another line about ⅜ to ½ inch (1 cm to 1.3 cm) below the first line. This is the tip of the nose. Using a slicing cut, form the slope of the nose up to your first stop cut at the bridge of the nose.

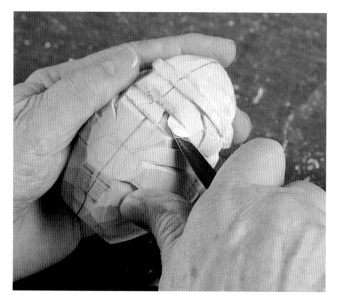

5 Mark vertical lines to designate the sides of the nose. Remove the areas on either side of the nose by slicing up to the stop cut at the brow line. You may have to deepen the brow line stop cut on both sides of the nose as well. This creates the area for the eyes.

7 Shape the beard and mustache area as one mass. You can carve the mustache separately if you like. Form the mouth by carving a deep triangular chip on the centerline.

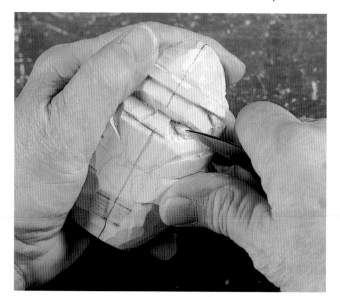

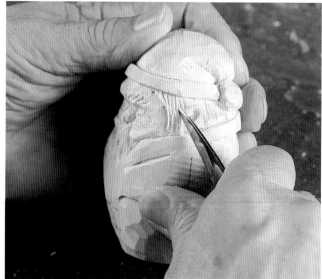

6 Draw the shape of the eyes. Check the eye locations. Are they the same size and on the same level? Use the tip of your knife to stop cut the upper and lower eyelids in an oval shape. Use your knife to remove a narrow slit for the pupils.

8 Use the knife or V-tool to texture the beard and mustache. Also texture the rest of the hair, and round over the cheeks and nose. Using the tip of your knife, round the corners of the ears and gouge out a small hole in the center. Use the #3 gouge to texture the cuffs and the fur trim on the jacket. You can sand for a smoother surface, but I like this Santa with an "as carved" surface along with a natural finish. If you want to paint your Santa, use thinned acrylic washes, and build up the coats until you have the color intensity you like.

Swimming Dolphins Plaque

Pierced carving is a variation of relief carving in which the background is completely removed by drilling or sawing through the full thickness of the wood. The filigree screens of India and the Middle East are intricate examples of this style of carving. The beauty of this technique lies in its simplicity and elegant curving lines.

YOU WILL NEED

Basswood, ⅜ x 6½ x 11 inches (1 x 16.5 x 27.9 cm)	#7 gouge, ⅝ inch (1.6 cm) wide
Bench hook, clamped to work surface	Riffler file
Drill, with a ¼-inch (6 mm) bit	Eye tool or nail set (optional)
Fixed-blade carving knife	Cloth-backed abrasive, sandpaper, or open abrasive (150 to 320 grit)
Coping saw or jigsaw (optional)	Desired finish

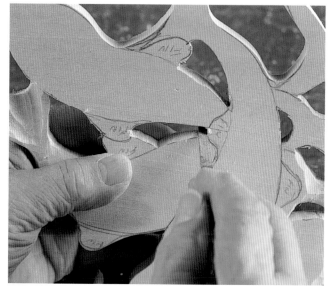

1 Transfer the pattern on page 79 to the wood, and cut your blank. The grain of the wood should run lengthwise to the design. Drill holes between the fish where you'll remove the waste wood. The drilled holes speed up the process considerably. Place the blank in the bench hook, and use the knife to remove the drilled-through waste wood. You could also use a coping saw or jigsaw and a fret board.

3 Use the riffler file to clean out the areas where you've removed waste wood.

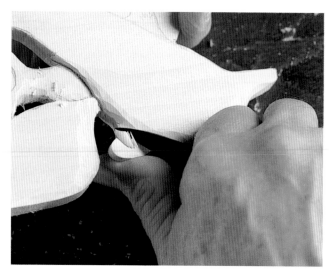

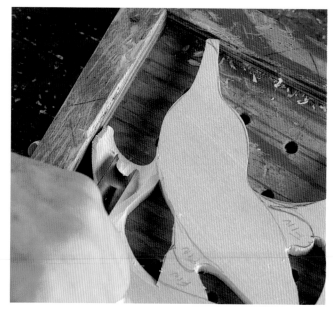

2 Round over the edges and develop the basic shape of each fish. You may wish to mark the fins at this point so you won't inadvertently cut them off. With the knife, use a rolling and slicing cut to curve the fins. You can also use a #7 gouge.

4 With the #7 gouge, develop the curves in each of the tails. Little or no detailing is required with this carving. You may want to add eyes with an eye tool or nail set. Just push the tool into the wood at the appropriate spot. Sand the whole piece smooth, progressing from 150- to 320-grit abrasive. Let the abrasive do the work; don't press too hard, and sand with the grain as much as possible. Finish as desired.

Standing Bear

The bear is a favorite subject for carvers, and as with any subject, the more you know about it, the better your carving will be. Check the library, collect pictures, and research bears as much as you can before carving. Anatomy is important—the bear, like all animals, is built around a skeleton, to which muscles and skin are attached. The joints are joined together and slant at similar angles. A knowledge of how they all work together is vital to a good carving.

YOU WILL NEED

Basswood or white pine, 2½ x 3½ x 6 inches (6.4 x 8.9 x 15.2 cm)	#3 gouge, ¼ inch (6 mm) wide
Fixed-blade carving knife	#11 gouge, ¼ inch (6 mm) wide
70° V-tool gouge, ¼ inch (6 mm) wide	Woodburning tool (optional)
	Desired finish

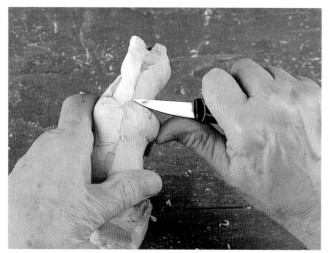

1 Transfer the patterns on page 79 to a squared piece of wood, and cut your blank. The grain of the wood should run the vertical length of the bear. Note that the head is turned at a slight angle. Use the knife to round over and block out the basic shape. The body has three main sections, the shoulder area, the stomach, and the hips. The backbone is relatively straight. Bears are large with a lot of bulk that hangs in wrinkles and folds. In the shaping stage, you want to block out the basic widths and planes, and mark the high points (shoulder and hip joints) first so that you don't carve away too much wood. Begin from the back and work around to the front.

2 At the shoulders, start about ⅛ inch (3 mm) on either side of your centerline, and leave this area high and flat. If you carve off the centerline be sure to re-mark it. This will help you keep the bear symmetrical. The front should be a little heavier and sag slightly.

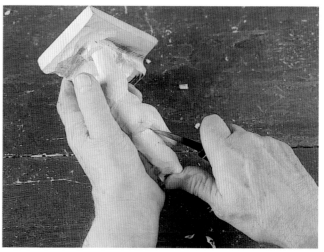

3 Use the V-tool or #11 gouge to shape the backs and fronts of the four legs close to the body by forming their outlines. Keep the legs squarish, and make the paws oversized to allow for the claws.

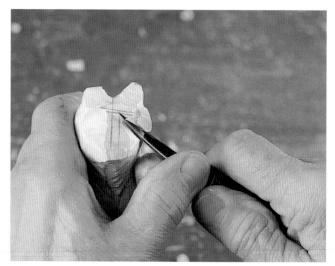

4 Block out the head with the knife. Remember that the ears are flush and at the side of the head. They're rounded and pointed at the rear of the head. The eyes are located halfway between the ears and the tip of the nose. Make a stop cut on both sides of the nose for the eye sockets, and keep the top of the nose flat. Make a slicing cut along the nose into your stop cut, forming a vertical area for the eye sockets.

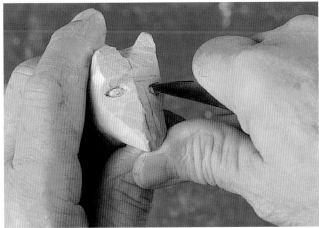

5 Draw in the eyes on this flat area, and check the symmetry. With the point of your knife, carve the eyes using a stop cut to form the upper and lower lids. Leave a little mound to form the pupils by removing a tiny triangular chip in the corners of the eyes.

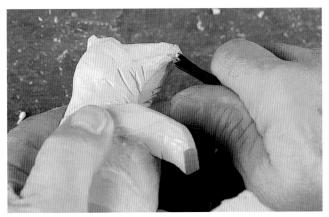

6 The mouth extends from a vertical line down from the eyes to the rear of the jaw. Draw the nostril area and stop cut around it lightly. Form the upper lip below the nostril, and round over the nose. Extend the upper lip with a V-cut to form the lower lip. Check the nose area, and make sure the top of the nose is flat.

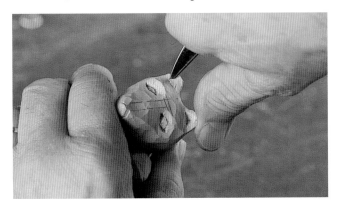

7 Finish rounding the ears, and form a flat surface on the fronts of the ears, tapering and rounding

them to the rear. Use the tip of your knife or a gouge to hollow the area in the front of each ear.

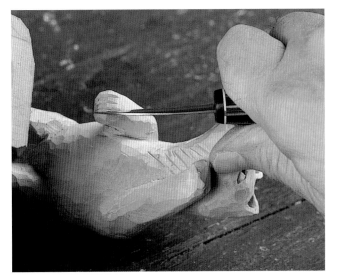

8 Draw and shape the paws and claws.

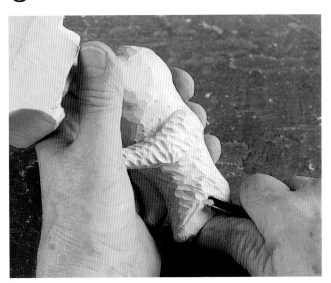

9 Mark the hairline tracts forming a slight ridge from the shoulders to the paws on each side. Use the veiner or the #3 gouge to create the look of hair, by making small scoops over all the body. These gouge marks should follow the hair tracts and flow lines of the body. Use smaller gouge marks on the head. Also, don't create as many marks for the head. Keep your gouge moving, and don't concentrate too long in any one area. Use the knife and #11 gouge to make the base look like a rocky ledge. No sanding is needed. Your gouge marks should leave smooth surfaces all over the bear's body. Finish as desired.

Paperweight

*This dogwood relief paperweight is in the form of a classic design called a roundel,
which is an architectural carving in a flat, round ornamental style, similar to ones used
during the Gothic period in England.*

YOU WILL NEED

Butternut, cherry, walnut, or other
hardwood, ¾ x 3 inches (1.9 x 7.6 cm)
in diameter

Bench hook, clamped to work surface

Fixed-blade carving knife

60° V-tool gouge, ¼ inch (6 mm) wide

Assorted carving gouges (#3, #5, #7,
#8, #11)

Riffler files

Desired finish

Large, 2-inch-diameter (5.1 cm) washer

Glue

Felt

1 Transfer the patterns on page 79 to the wood, and cut your blank. Place the blank in the bench hook, and use the knife or V-tool to outline the center circle and the petals with a series of stop cuts.

2 In relief carving, you should select your gouges to fit the shapes of the design (petals). This produces a sharp, clean outline. Use the gouges as noted on the template on page 79, and switch gouges to carve each of the different elements of the outline.

3 Using the #7 gouge, cut into the stop cut you made on the center circle. You're only removing about ⅛ inch (3 mm), so don't over cut. Slope your gouge away from the center so you don't undercut the circle and chance chipping it out completely. Continue using the #5 and #7 gouges to stop cut the outline of the petals. Remember to make your cross-grain cuts first.

4 Use the #7 and #8 gouges to remove the wood around the center, and taper the petals about 3/16

inch (5 mm) into the stop cut around the center. Slope the stop cuts away from the petals. Be careful not to use too much pressure at the outer edges; the cross-grain can break out very easily. Don't pry; make clean slicing cuts.

5 Use the knife and small micro-gouges to lower the background between the petals and around the flower out to the outer edge. Don't undercut the petals at this stage. To carve the berries, cross-hatch the center circle at right angles with the V-tool and round over the corners with the knife. Now use the knife and gouges to undercut the petals lightly, and create shadows for depth. Sand the background to a smooth finish. You may need to use a riffler file to get into the small areas between the petals to remove all the fuzz.

6 Finish as desired. Antiquing the paperweight will give it an old look. Follow manufacturer's directions, or use a dark stain, rubbing off the excess to produce highlights. Hollow out the underside of the paperweight with a gouge or the knife, and glue the washer in place. Then cut out the felt and glue it to the bottom, covering the washer.

Cat Mirror

This carving is really a type of relief carving called half-round.
You might be inspired to try something different with this design, so let your imagination
go wild on your next version of this fun project.

YOU WILL NEED

Basswood or white pine, 1½ x 8 x 9 inches (3.8 x 20.3 x 22.9 cm)	Mirror
Drill	Cloth-backed abrasive, sandpaper, or open abrasive (120, 220, and 320 grit)
Bench hook, clamped to work surface	
#3 gouge, 1½ inches (3.8 cm) wide	Primer
Fixed-blade carving knife	Acrylic paints
Vise	Woodburning tool (optional)
Saw	Brads
#7 gouge or chisel	Picture frame hanger

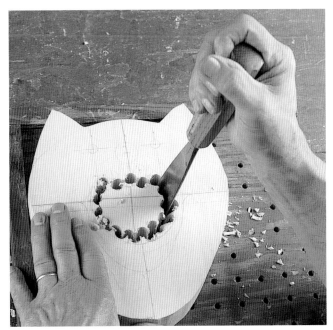

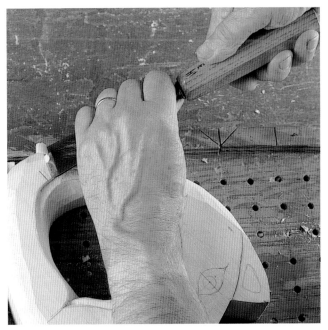

1 Transfer the pattern on page 80 to a squared piece of wood, and cut your blank. The grain of the wood should run the vertical length of the face. Note: the teeth are not cut out at this stage. Drill holes in the mouth area to aid in removing the waste wood. Use the bench hook to secure the wood while carving.

3 Use the #3 gouge to remove the waste wood while developing the basic shape.

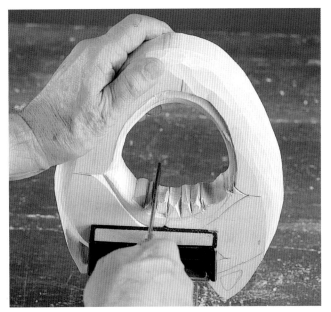

2 With the knife, stop cut along the outline of the lips, about 3/16 inch (5 mm) deep. Remove the waste wood from the inside of the lip to the stop cut to form the lips.

4 Place the cat in a vise. Establish the level of the teeth by lowering the wood in the tooth area, the mouth corners, and the lower lip. Redraw the teeth on the proper level, and use the saw to stop cut between the teeth. Carve out the waste wood between the teeth with the knife.

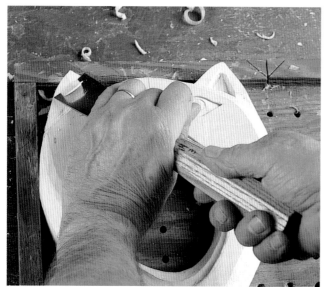

5 Develop the basic level and shape of the ears by removing the waste wood about ½ inch (1.3 cm). With the #3 gouge, round the ears from the back slightly so they tip forward.

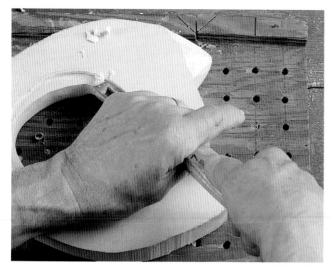

6 Turn the carving over and with the #7 gouge or chisel, remove waste wood about ¼ inch deep (6 mm) for the mirror.

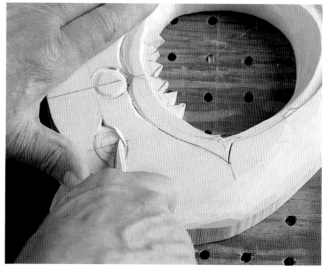

7 Sketch in the eyes. Check the alignment and size to be sure they look right and are the same size and level. Stop cut along the line of the upper and lower lids with the knife. Thrust the point of your knife into the corners of the eyes, creating stop cuts. Now, remove a three-sided chip from the corners with the knife, and round over the pupil area down into the corners. Make the eyeballs as smooth as possible.

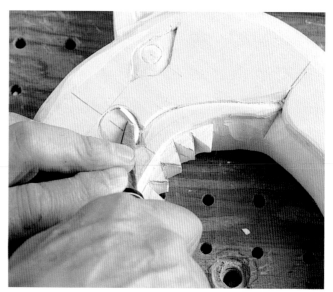

8 Stop cut around the nose, and round it over. Use 120-grit abrasive to remove your initial knife and gouge cuts, smoothing the entire surface. Finish sanding using 220- and 320-grit abrasives. This project really needs to be painted. Select the colors you like, and use acrylic paints and maybe a coat of primer or gesso. Darken the areas around the mouth and ears, add eyebrows, a nose, eyelashes, and whiskers. You can also use a woodburning tool to shade and color the cat. Add the mirror, secure it with brads, and add a hanger.

Stylized Hummingbird

Carving a realistic bird requires an intimate knowledge of the bird's size, color, feathers, flight patterns, nesting habits, etc. This takes a lot of research and study. This hummingbird is carved in what I call "stylized realism." That is, its size and proportions are correct, but the feather details are not required for you to recognize it as lifelike (though stylized carvings do require considerable time to produce the smooth finish).

Basswood, 1½ x 3½ x 5 inches (3.8 x 8.9 x 12.7 cm)

Fixed-blade carving knife

½-inch (1.3 cm) drum sander

Cloth-backed abrasive, sandpaper, or open abrasive (320 and 400 grit)

Flexible plastic abrasive pads (gray or white)

Desired finish

Screw eye

String

Drill (optional)

Branch (optional)

22-gauge wire (optional)

1 Transfer the patterns on page 80 to a squared piece of wood, and cut your blank. The grain of the wood should run the length of the bird. With the knife, round over the edges and develop the body, wings, and tail. Be careful on your cross-grain cuts so you don't snap off portions of the wings or tail.

2 Carefully shape the head with the knife. Remember, birds have smoothly sloping necks. A

good way to check your symmetry is to look at your carving in a mirror. Taper the beak using slicing and paring cuts with the knife, but leave ample wood for the final sanding.

3 With the basic shape established, use a 180-grit abrasive in the ½-inch (1.3 cm) drum sander to develop the final smooth contours of the body, wings, and tail. Remember, sand with the grain as much as possible. When all of the knife marks are gone, examine the bird closely. Since it's stylized, almost no detailing is required, though the smooth finish must reflect the realistic shape and action of a real hummingbird in flight. Remove any fuzz, and polish your bird with 320- and 400-grit abrasives.

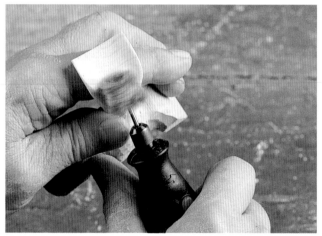

4 Use the flexible plastic abrasive buffs in your power tool to get a really smooth overall finish. When you're satisfied with your finish, apply a coat of sanding sealer. After the sealer coat is dry, buff again to remove any raised grain. Finish as desired. Either hang the hummingbird with a screw eye and string or drill a small hole in the bottom of the bird to mount it on the branch with a piece of the 22-gauge wire.

Spirit Face Hiking Staff

Hikers use staffs to maneuver rough terrain and ford streams. Hiking staffs come in all kinds of materials these days; however, a carved hiking staff commands special recognition on the trail. At home, they become conversation pieces and even family heirlooms.

YOU WILL NEED

Sourwood, maple, dogwood, birch, or spruce sapling, 1¼ inches (3.2 cm) in diameter and 5 feet (1.5 m) long

#3 gouge, 1½ inches (3.8 cm) wide

#11 veiner gouge, ¼ inch (6 mm) wide

Fixed-blade carving knife

Nail set

V-tool gouge, ¼ inch (6 mm) wide

Woodburning tool (optional)

Drill, with ¼-inch (6 mm) bit

Desired finish

Rubber or metal tip

1 Find a piece of wood that'll work for your staff. If your wood is freshly cut, it'll be easier to carve than older air-dried wood. Be sure it's fairly straight. Clean off the bark from the top 12 inches (30.5 cm) of your staff with the #3 gouge. You don't need to remove all the bark. Mark a centerline and trace the patterns on page 80 onto the wood. Then mark a horizontal line for the brow line about ¾ inch (1.9 cm) below the top of the staff. Mark another horizontal line about ¾ inch (1.9 cm) below the first line. This is the tip of the nose. Then, cut two horizontal grooves about ¼ inch (6 mm) deep on the two lines drawn across the face area. With the #3 gouge, round over the top of the staff.

3 Use the knife to slope the nose from the tip up to the bridge at the bottom of your first cut and form the browline.

4 Make a stop cut at the tip of the nose, and notch back to remove the wood under the cheekbones, forming the top of the mustache.

2 With the #11 veiner, create an outline of the facial area. Mark two vertical lines either side of the nose. Then, with the veiner, remove the wood on either side of the vertical nose lines.

5 Sketch the lower edge of the mustache, and stop cut it about ¼ inch (6 mm) deep. Round over the

mustache, sloping it back into the upper edge of the mustache.

6 Begin detailing by removing a deep triangular chip below the center of the mustache to create the mouth. Use the #3 gouge or the knife to shape the lower lip below the mouth opening.

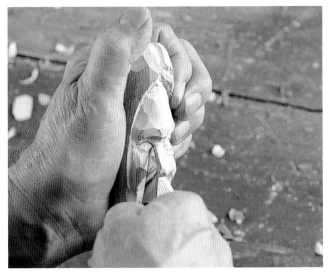

7 Round over the nose with the knife, and form the nose wings. Don't undercut the nostrils. Form the nostrils and flair them slightly. Pare down the cheek areas and smooth the lower cheekline. Round the forehead above the eyebrows back to the facial outline. Use the veiner to create the crease between the eyebrows above the nose.

8 Use the #11 gouge to round the eye sockets. Start at the centerline of each eye, and form the corners about ⅛ inch (3 mm) deeper. Sketch in your eyes. Be sure they're level and of equal size. Stop cut the upper and lower eyelids. Use the tip of the knife to remove a triangular chip in the corners. If you want him to look to the side, take a larger chip out of one side, and the eye will look to the other side. Round over the pupil, and add a circle using a nail set to form the pupil.

9 Use the V-tool to form the hair part. Just try to create the overall waves and flow lines of the hair out from the part and over and down the top of the staff. These first cuts should be fairly deep, about ¼ inch (6 mm). Now sketch in the mustache and beard flow lines. With the basic shape of the hair created, use the knife, V-tool, or woodburning tool to create the individual hair lines. Remember, hair is not straight, so keep your tool moving in graceful curves. Drill a ¼-inch (6 mm) hole through the hair area for a carrying loop. Finish the staff as desired. Add a rubber or metal tip to the bottom of the staff.

Old Shoe

The old shoe is a timeless carving project. I've seen some full-sized carved shoes that are so realistic that,
until you picked it up, you couldn't tell it wasn't the real thing.
High-button shoes, ski boots, and hiking shoes of all kinds have also been carved.
When you select the wood for your shoe, be sure the grain runs parallel to the sole.

Basswood or butternut, 2 x 3 x 5 inches (5.1 x 7.6 x 12.7 cm)

Drill, with ⅞-inch (2.2 cm) Forstner-type and ⅛-inch (3 mm) bits

Fixed-blade carving knife

Curved knife or #7 or #9 gouges, ⅝ inch (1.6 cm) wide

Drum sander

Desired finish

Leather lace

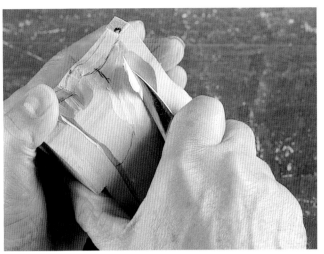

2 Use the knife to round off the back corners of the heel. Use a rolling cut to form the concave areas of the sides. You may want to make the sides flare slightly at the top.

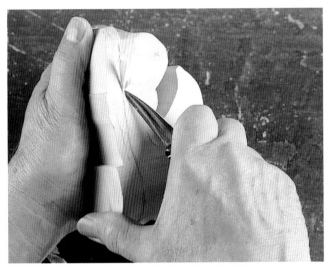

1 Transfer the patterns on page 77 to a squared piece of wood. Before you cut out your blank, mark the centerline on the top, and measure 1 inch (2.5 cm) from the back edge of the shoe. Drill a ⅞-inch (2.2 cm) hole, 2 inches (5.1 cm) deep. Now, cut your blank and remove the waste wood to form the basic shoe. Use care in removing the waste wood between the toe and the tongue. Mark the top edge of the sole all around the shoe. Use the knife to stop cut along the line about ⅛ inch (3 mm) deep. Make a slicing cut at about 45° to the stop cut from above the sole.

3 Draw a clearance line ⅛ inch (3 mm) inside the top of the shoe, and with the curved knife or #7 or #9 gouge, rough out the waste wood inside the boot.

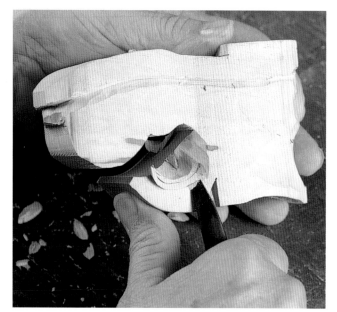

4 Round over the toe and the underside of the tongue with the knife, using rolling and slicing cuts. These cuts will help develop the shape.

5 Remove the rest of the wood on the inside of the boot and tongue with the drum sander. You can also do this step with a knife or curved knife.

6 With the basic form established, you can begin the detailing phase by stop cutting the seam areas at the back of the heel and in the lace areas. Create a raised seam area by paring down the heel and sides slightly at the seam line. An old boot is not symmetrical, so develop a well-worn look and add creases to the toe with the knife.

7 Carefully mark your lace holes, and drill them with the ⅛-inch (3 mm) drill bit through the sides. Sand and finish as desired. This piece was stained and protected with two coats of lacquer. Add a leather lace for a final touch.

Crocodile Slide Whistle

Simple whistles have always been delightful to carve. You can carve one out of a twig of river willow by removing the bark and creating a hollow sound chamber. Then you carve a mouthpiece and an angled hole, and replace the bark. Here's one whistle that's special not only because it can play more than one note (it's a slide whistle!), but also because, well, it's a crocodile!

YOU WILL NEED

Basswood, 2 x 1¾ x 10 inches (5.1 x 4.4 x 25.4 cm)

Drill, with a 10-inch-long (25.4 cm), ⁵⁄₁₆-inch (8 mm) bit

Fixed-blade carving knife

#3 gouge, ½ inch (1.3 cm) wide

Birch dowel, ⁵⁄₁₆ inch (8 mm) in diameter and 7 inches (17.8 cm) long

70° V-tool gouge, ¼ inch (6 mm) wide

Backsaw

Carpenter's glue

Cloth-backed abrasive, sandpaper, or open abrasive (180, 220, and 320 grit)

Woodburning tool (optional)

Desired finish

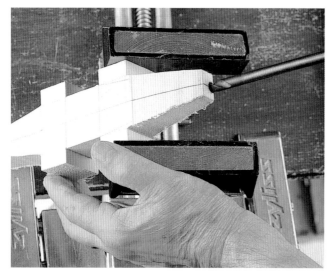

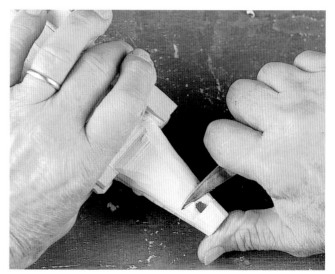

1 Transfer the patterns on page 77 to a squared piece of wood. The grain of the wood should run the length of the piece. Cut out the blank. Mark the centerlines on the mouth end, and drill a ⁵⁄₁₆-inch (8 mm) hole for the mouth (whistle opening) with the 10-inch-long (25.4 cm) drill bit. Drill all the way into the tail section so that you can secure the dowel slide later.

3 With the knife, make a stop cut ½ inch (1.3 cm) in from the tip of the nose on the underside of the jaw. It should just go through to the drilled hole. Use a slicing cut to taper the underside of the jaw, cutting into the dowel hole. The tapered area should expose about ⅛ inch (3 mm) of the drilled hole.

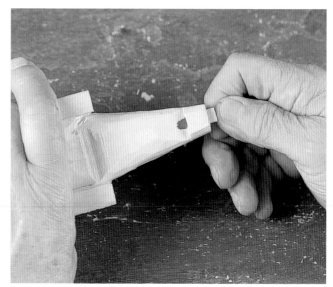

2 Use the knife to round over and form the basic shape of the body and legs. Stop cut the inside edge of the legs, and use the #3 gouge to remove the waste wood between the legs on the bottom of the blank down to the body.

4 Cut off a ½-inch-long (1.3 cm) piece of the dowel, and slice off a ⅛-inch (3 mm) sliver on one side only. Insert the ½-inch (1.3 cm) dowel into the mouth with the sliver side down to match up with the tapered whistle hole under the jaw.

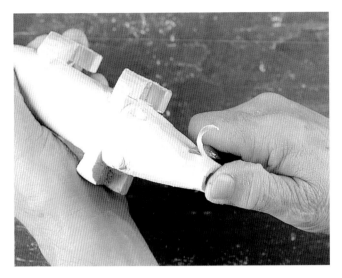

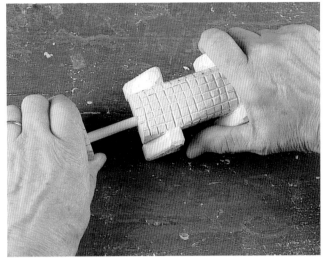

5 Round over the eyes, and carve the legs to size with the knife. Pare down the snout appropriately.

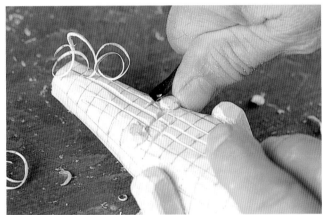

6 Draw lines the full length of your crocodile ¼ inch (6 mm) apart. Draw lines at right angles to the first set of lines, and space them ¼ inch (6 mm) apart to form tiny squares. Use the V-tool to incise the lines to give your crocodile a scaly appearance.

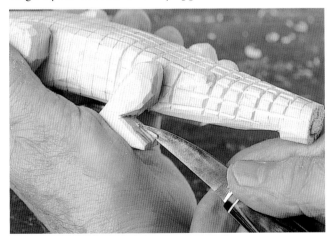

7 Carefully carve the toes and claws on each foot with the knife.

8 With the backsaw, cut the tail off just behind the rear legs. Glue a 6-inch-long (15.2 cm) piece of the dowel into the tail section. Sand and smooth the dowel until it slides easily into the body section. You will also need to clean out the hole with the drill from the tail end to facilitate the sliding action. Now try blowing into the whistle. You may have to adjust the mouth taper or the opening on the bottom to get a good sound. Move the slide while you're blowing it, and see how the tone changes. You may need to adjust the length of the dowel to get a proper tone when it's all the way in. Glue the short dowel in the mouth in place.

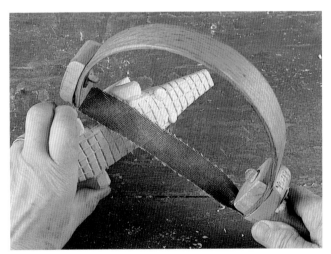

9 Sand the crocodile lightly with 180-grit abrasive to remove any pencil marks or fuzz. You may prefer to paint your crocodile. Use watered-down acrylic paint for a stained appearance, or build up coats to obtain the intensity of color you desire. Another interesting effect can be acquired by burning the scales and shading them with the woodburning tool.

Ahab

A caricature exaggerates human features, such as an expression, nose, feet, hands, etc., for comic effect. I like to carve miniature caricatures, but don't let that stop you from enlarging this pattern. What I like about this size is that I can carry it in my pocket and work on it at my leisure.

YOU WILL NEED

Basswood or white pine, 1¼ x 1½ x 4⅜ inches (3.2 x 3.8 x 11.2 cm)

Fixed-blade carving knife

Drill, with various bits

70° V-tool gouge, ¼ inch (6 mm) wide

Bamboo fondue skewer

Desired finish

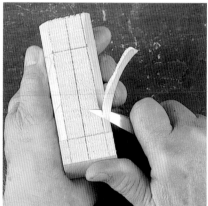

1 Transfer the patterns on page 77 to a squared piece of wood. The grain of the wood should run the vertical length of the body. Before you begin carving out the blank, first draw vertical lines on each corner ¼ inch (6 mm) from each edge. With the knife, trim off each of these corners down to the base.

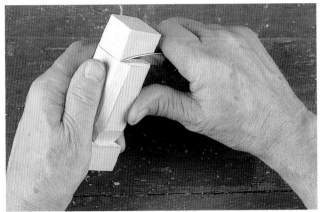

2 Start rounding with the knife at the top, and work your way down the piece. Small cuts are better than large ones on a carving this size. Create the shoulder area with a series of stop cuts. Make sure the shoulders are on the same level. If not, adjust your stop cuts.

3 Drill between and through the legs at the crotch and at the base. Develop the front and back of the pants with a series of stop cuts below the jacket. Cross-grain cuts are vulnerable, so make sure you make them deep enough, and don't pry with your knife. Slicing with your knife up under his rear end, remove the waste wood down to the top level of the base and the shoes.

4 Mark the arm positions, but don't carve them yet. With the V-tool, start carving on the back of the figure at both arms above the elbows.

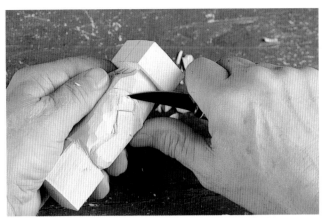

5 On the right arm, use the knife to make a stop cut down to the pocket line, forming the back of the sleeve. Let the pocket flare out so it bulges. (He's got his hand in his pocket!)

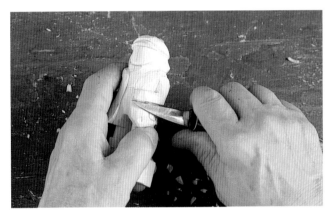

6 In carving the left arm, make sure to leave wood for the fist. Stop cut under the left forearm, wrist to elbow. Carefully slice into the stop cut from above the pocket and notch at the elbow. The pocket on this side does not bulge out as much as the one on the right.

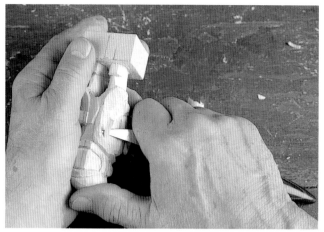

7 Make stop cuts above both arms in the front, and pare away the jacket. Deepen the cut at the elbows. Stop cut the jacket flap on the back, and pare up to undercut the back flap. Stop cut and create the jacket collar in the front.

8 Using the knife or V-tool, carve the horizontal stripes in the shirt. Stop cut the belt and fly areas of the pants. Remove any waste wood from the shoes with the knife. Slope the sides and flatten the top.

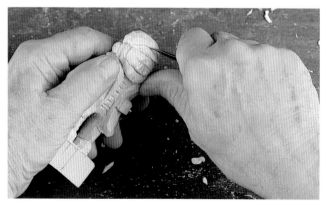

9 Draw the hat, hair, and beard outlines, and stop cut them about ⅛ inch (3 mm) deep with the knife. Carve the face details, (see pages 64 and 65, steps 2 through 8 for guidelines). Don't carve away the lapels, and round the stubby neck area to let the beard stand out. With the knife, round the cheeks and mouth area, stop cut the mouth, and deepen the corners. Form the bill and the drooping top with its ball. Use the V-tool or knife to texture the hair and beard.

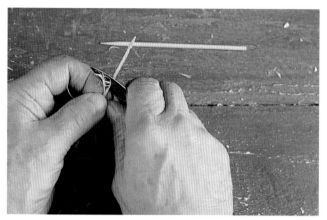

10 Carefully drill the hole through the fist of the left hand for the harpoon. You may have to remove part of the jacket so the harpoon will reach the base. Carve the harpoon from the bamboo fondue skewer. Thin down the shaft and add a point.

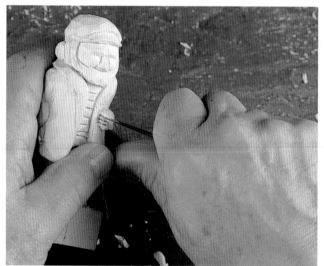

11 To carve the left hand, form the surface planes of the fingers and then divide them in half. Then divide each half remaining in half, and you'll have four fingers. Taper the hand into the cuff. Be sure you carve a cuff on the other sleeve above the pocket. Groove and texture the eyebrows, and shape the area above the eyebrows up to the cap. Incise the name on the front of the base. Finish as desired.

Carved Egg

Faberge isn't the only one who can create an egg masterpiece—you can relief carve a unique gift or ornament out of a wooden egg. You can find wooden eggs in woodcarving catalogs and some hobby and craft shops. Some carvers make heads out of wooden eggs, though I prefer to carve scenes. You can hang your egg or mount it onto a base.

YOU WILL NEED

Basswood, cedar, birch, or other wooden egg, 2 x 2½ inches (5.1 x 6.4 cm)	#3 fishtail palm gouge (optional)
#11 veiner gouge, ⅛ inch (3 mm) wide	Desired finish
Fixed-blade carving knife	Screw eye (to hang the egg)
V-tool, ¼ inch (6 mm) wide (optional)	Drill (optional)
Small detail knife or Kolrosing knife	16-gauge copper wire (optional)
	Mounting block (optional)

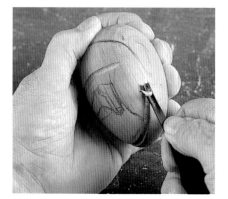

1 Sketch an outline frame for your design on the edge (striped) side of your egg. Carving on the smooth side can result in portions of the design splitting off. Size the design on page 77 to fit the framed area. Make sure your perspective is right, then sketch the house and chimney inside the framed area. Use the #11 gouge to outline the framed area. Carve about ³/₁₆ inch (5 mm) deep along the frame line.

2 Begin the shaping phase by establishing the outside face of the chimney with the knife or the #3 fishtail palm gouge.

3 Use the knife to carve the end of the cabin.

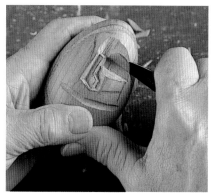

4 Remove the waste wood behind and above the cabin, and begin establishing the slope of the roof. Finish carving the cabin walls, roof, and chimney, maintaining the perspective by tapering the cabin into the egg.

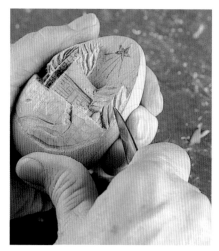

5 Carve the trees using the knife or V-tool. Don't forget to carve the trunks. You may want to use a rotary power tool and carving bits to carve the trunks.

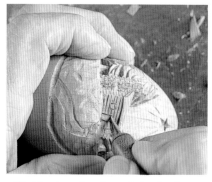

6 Having developed the basic shape, use the small detail knife to inscribe the door, windows, logs in the cabin, and the rocks in the chimney. Carve the path to the door. Remove any remaining wood in the background (from above cabin, under trees, etc.).

7 Incise the star and rays in the background. I prefer to leave this design "as carved," but you may want to sand some areas for smoothness or to remove some "fuzz." Finish as desired. Use a screw eye to hang the egg, or mount the egg on a base. Drill a hole for your mounting wire, and use 16-gauge copper wire to attach the egg to the block.

Patterns

Enlarge each pattern 200-percent on a photocopier. You can also scan the patterns and enlarge them on your computer before printing them.

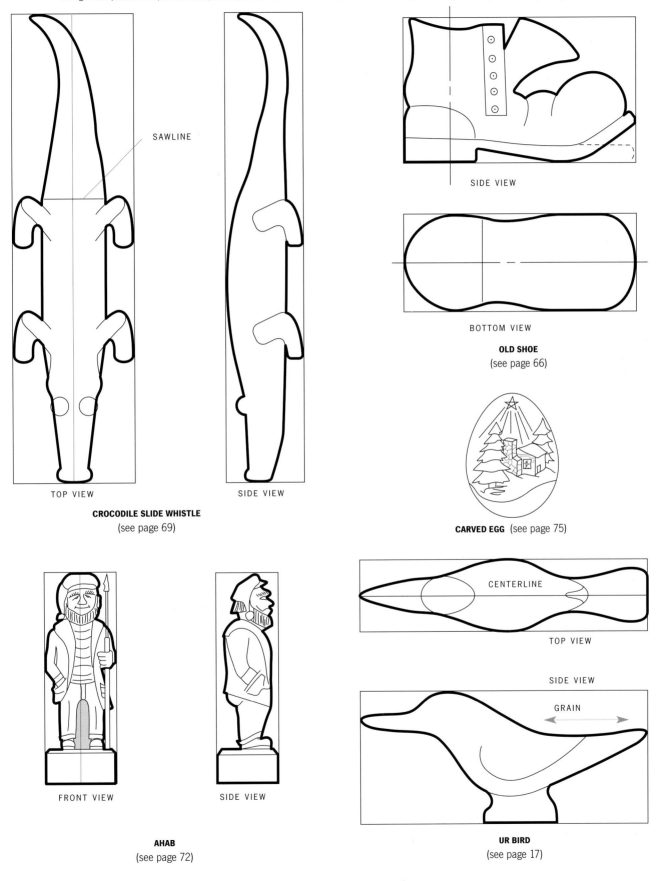

SAWLINE

TOP VIEW

SIDE VIEW

CROCODILE SLIDE WHISTLE
(see page 69)

SIDE VIEW

BOTTOM VIEW

OLD SHOE
(see page 66)

CARVED EGG (see page 75)

FRONT VIEW

SIDE VIEW

AHAB
(see page 72)

CENTERLINE

TOP VIEW

SIDE VIEW

GRAIN

UR BIRD
(see page 17)

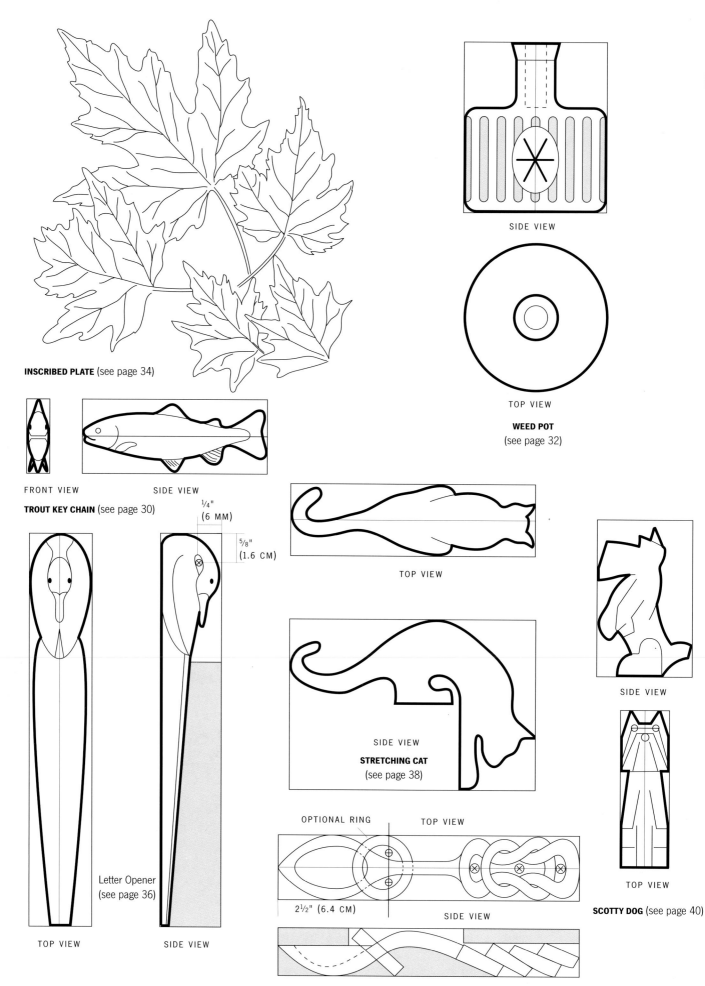

INSCRIBED PLATE (see page 34)

SIDE VIEW

TOP VIEW

WEED POT
(see page 32)

FRONT VIEW   SIDE VIEW

TROUT KEY CHAIN (see page 30)

¼"
(6 MM)

⅝"
(1.6 CM)

TOP VIEW

Letter Opener
(see page 36)

TOP VIEW   SIDE VIEW

SIDE VIEW
STRETCHING CAT
(see page 38)

SIDE VIEW

TOP VIEW

SCOTTY DOG (see page 40)

OPTIONAL RING   TOP VIEW

2½" (6.4 CM)

SIDE VIEW

LOVE SPOON (see page 45)

MINIATURE MASK (see page 43)

TOP VIEW

SIDE VIEW

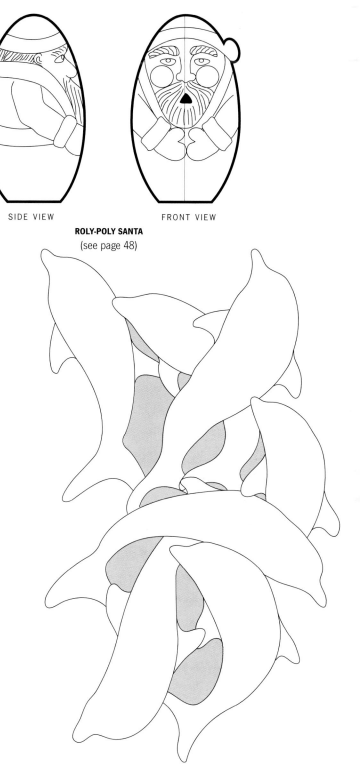

SIDE VIEW

FRONT VIEW

ROLY-POLY SANTA
(see page 48)

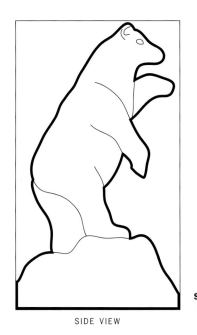

SIDE VIEW

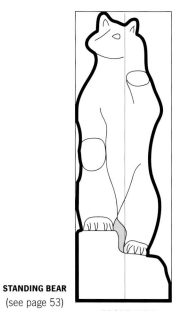

STANDING BEAR
(see page 53)

FRONT VIEW

SWIMMING DOLPHINS PLAQUE
Gray areas indicate waste wood (see page 51).

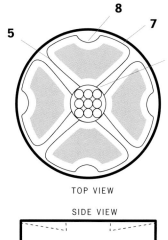

8

7

5

11

TOP VIEW

PAPERWEIGHT
The numbers correspond to the gouge you
should use for the areas indicated.
(see page 56)

SIDE VIEW

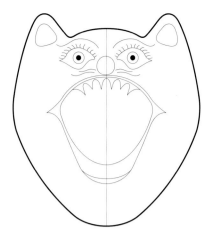

CAT MIRROR
(see page 58) ENLARGE 400%

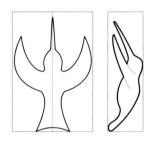

TOP VIEW   SIDE VIEW

STYLIZED HUMMINGBIRD
(see page 61) ENLARGE 400%

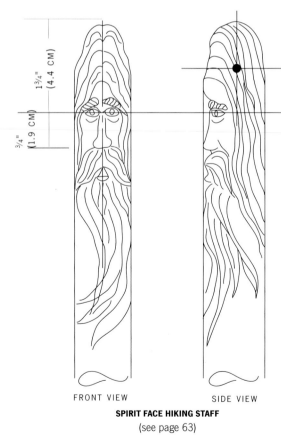

$1\frac{3}{4}$"
(4.4 CM)

$\frac{3}{4}$"
(1.9 CM)

FRONT VIEW   SIDE VIEW

SPIRIT FACE HIKING STAFF
(see page 63)

Index

A Note About Suppliers

Usually, the supplies you need for making the projects in Lark books can be found at your local craft supply store, discount mart, home improvement center, or retail shop relevant to the topic of the book. Occasionally, however, you may need to buy materials or tools from specialty suppliers. In order to provide you with the most up-to-date information, we have created suppliers listings on our Web site, which we update on a regular basis. Visit us at www.larkbooks.com, click on "Craft Supply Sources," and then click on the relevant topic. You will find numerous companies listed with their web address and/or mailing address and phone number.

Contributing Gallery Artists

* Wayne Barton is the founder of The Alpine School of Woodcarving, Ltd., which is dedicated to the teaching of chip carving. <www.chipcarving.com>

* Don Burgdorf is an award-winning carver and artist. <www.artofdon.com>

* Robert G. Foulkes is a woodcarver who took his first woodcarving class from John Hillyer. 828-277-7723.

* Desiree Hajny, is an author, teacher, and woodcarver whose work can be found in all 50 states and six foreign countries. <www.dmea.net/~hajny/>

* Nicholas Herrera is a New Mexico native whose sculpture appears in collections including the Smithsonian National Gallery of American Art. Cavin-Morris Gallery, 560 Broadway, NY, NY 10012, (212) 226-3768.

* Drew Langsner is co-founder of Country Workshops and author of five woodcarving books. <www.countryworkshops.org>

* David Maggard is a woodcarver in Asheville, NC. <cdmaggard@earthlink.net>

* Ted Nichols hand carves collectibles and toys. <www.noahs-ark.com>

* "Woodbutcher" Jan Oegema is a woodcarver and carving teacher in Bowmanville, Ontario, Canada. <www.members.home.net/jancarves>

* Roy K. Pace carves original designs in his home in Greenbrier, TN. (615) 643-7967.

* Ron Ramsey is the third-generation carver who specializes in carved doors, mantels, architectural elements, and sculpture. <www.carvedbyramsey.com>

* Gail Stanek specializes in highly detailed hand-carved songbirds in wood.

<www.naturalimages.homestead.com>

* Alice Strom specializes in hand-painted folk art wood carvings. Spirit of America, Rt. 2 Box 358A, Nevis, MN 56467.